Master the Money Game: Wealth Accumulation Strategies

About the book

Master the Money Game: Wealth Accumulation Strategies serves as an essential guide for achieving financial success in today's complex economy. The book provides a step-by-step framework that starts with setting SMART financial goals and milestones. Each chapter addresses key topics for building wealth, beginning with the creation of a strategic plan for wealth accumulation. It further explores understanding market trends to enable informed decision-making and highlights methods for identifying profitable opportunities in the market. This structured approach aims to equip readers with the knowledge and skills needed for successful investing. Whether you're an individual looking to boost your finances or a business aiming for growth, this book provides the tools you need to navigate your financial journey effectively.

Author

Table of Contents

Chapter 1: Defining Clear Financial Goals and Milestones

Chapter 2: Developing a Strategic Plan for Wealth Accumulation

Chapter 3: Monitoring Progress and Adjusting Strategies

Chapter 4: Understanding Basic Financial Concepts

Chapter 5: Staying Updated on Market Trends

Chapter 6: Identifying Market Gaps and Opportunities

Chapter 7: Developing Innovative Products and Services

Chapter 8: Leveraging Digital Platforms for Scalability

Chapter 9: Diversifying Investments Across Asset Classes

Chapter 10: Long-term Growth and Income Strategies

Chapter 11: Upgrading with Technological Advancements

Chapter 12: Exploring Emerging Sectors

Chapter 13: Investing in Disruptive Innovations

Chapter 14: Building a Strong Professional Network

Chapter 15: Developing Effective Communication and Negotiation Skills

Chapter 16: Evaluating Investment Risks

Chapter 17: Implementing Risk Mitigation Strategies

Chapter 18: Preparing for Economic Downturns

Chapter 19: Exploring International Markets

Chapter 20: Adapting to Consumer Preferences and Market Dynamics

Chapter 1: Defining Clear Financial Goals and Milestone

Introduction

In the journey to financial success, defining clear financial goals and milestones is like charting a course on a map; it transforms your dreams into actionable steps. This chapter will guide you through the process of setting SMART goals—Specific, Measurable, Achievable, Relevant, and Time-bound—that provide a solid foundation for your financial aspirations. We'll explore how breaking down your ambitions into manageable milestones not only keeps you motivated but also helps you monitor your progress, ensuring that every step you take is aligned with your long-term vision. Whether you're an individual eager to boost your finances or a business striving for growth, establishing these goals will empower you to take control of your financial future with confidence and clarity.

Mastering Financial Clarity: Setting SMART Goals for Growth

When it comes to boosting your finances or driving business growth, clarity is key. In this discussion, we will explore the art of setting clear financial goals and creating milestones that serve as stepping stones toward achieving those goals. By applying the SMART framework—Specific, Measurable, Achievable, Relevant, and Time-bound—you can chart a path that not only guides your decisions but also keeps you motivated and accountable.

Understanding the SMART Framework

A) Specific

A specific goal is clear and unambiguous. Instead of saying, "I want to save money," a specific goal would be, "I want to save $5,000 for a family vacation." This clarity helps you focus your efforts and understand exactly what you're working towards.

Example: If you're a business owner, instead of aiming for "more customers," set a goal like, "I want to acquire 50 new customers in the next quarter."

B) Measurable

Measurable goals allow you to track your progress. This means establishing criteria that help you quantify your success.

Example: Instead of saying, "I want to improve my sales," say, "I want to increase my monthly sales by 20% over the next six months." This way, you can assess your progress and make adjustments as necessary.

C) Achievable

While it's great to aim high, your goals must also be realistic. An achievable goal is one that you can reasonably expect to accomplish given your resources and constraints.

Example: If your current savings rate is $100 a month, a goal to save $1,000 in one month may not be feasible. Instead, aim for saving $300 a month, leading to a more attainable total of $1,000 in just over three months.

D) Relevant

Your financial goals should align with your broader life or business objectives. A relevant goal will resonate with your values and aspirations, ensuring that you remain motivated.

Example: If your long-term goal is to retire comfortably, a relevant short-term goal could be, "I will contribute $500 monthly to my retirement account."

E) Time-bound

Establishing a deadline creates urgency and helps you stay focused. Without a timeline, goals can become indefinite and easily forgotten.

Example: Rather than stating, "I want to pay off my credit card debt," a time-bound goal would be, "I will pay off my credit card debt of $2,000 in the next eight months."

Creating Milestones

Once you've established your SMART goals, the next step is to break them down into manageable milestones. These milestones act as checkpoints on your journey, providing opportunities to celebrate small victories and recalibrate if necessary.

A) Benefits of Milestones

1. Enhanced Motivation: Achieving milestones provides a sense of accomplishment that fuels further progress.

Example: If your goal is to save $5,000 for a vacation, celebrate reaching the $1,000 mark with a small reward. This reinforces your commitment and encourages you to keep going.

2. Progress Tracking: Milestones allow you to measure how far you've come, making it easier to see if you're on track.

Example: In business, if your goal is to increase sales by 20% in six months, set monthly sales targets to track your progress toward that 20%.

3. **Adjustability**: If you find that you're falling behind on a milestone, it gives you the chance to reassess your strategies and make necessary adjustments.

Example: If you aimed to save $1,000 in three months but only saved $600, you can adjust your future savings plans to meet your ultimate goal.

Effective Strategies for Goal Achievement

1. Visualize Your Goals

Creating a visual representation of your goals can significantly enhance your commitment. Use vision boards, charts, or apps that illustrate your objectives and milestones.

Benefit: Visual cues serve as constant reminders of what you're working towards, keeping you motivated and focused.

2. Develop an Action Plan

Once your goals are set, outline actionable steps to achieve them. Break down each goal into smaller tasks that can be tackled over time.

Example: If your goal is to save $5,000, your action plan might include:

a) Setting up an automatic transfer of $400 to a savings account each month.

b) Cutting back on discretionary spending by 20%.

3. Regularly Review and Adjust

Set aside time each month to review your progress. Are you on track with your milestones? If not, what can be improved?

Benefit: Regular reviews keep you accountable and provide opportunities to adjust your strategies to stay aligned with your goals.

4. Break Down Larger Goals into Short-Term Objectives

Large financial goals can feel overwhelming, so it's beneficial to break them into smaller, more manageable short-term objectives. This makes the overall goal less daunting and helps maintain momentum.

Example: If your ultimate goal is to save $10,000 for a home down payment, break it down into quarterly savings objectives of $2,500. This way, you can celebrate smaller successes along the way, keeping your motivation high.

5. Create a Reward System

Incentivize your progress by establishing a reward system for achieving milestones. This approach makes the journey more enjoyable and reinforces positive behaviours.

Example: If you reach a milestone—like saving $2,000—treat yourself to a small celebration, such as a nice dinner or a weekend getaway. These rewards not only motivate you to stay focused but also help you appreciate the effort you're putting into achieving your goals.

Summary

Setting clear financial goals and defining milestones is not just a matter of numbers; it's about creating a vision for your future. By using the SMART framework and implementing effective strategies, you can transform your aspirations into tangible results. Whether you're an individual looking to improve your financial health or a business aiming for growth, taking these steps will set you on a path to success. Remember, each milestone you achieve is a testament to your dedication and commitment to your financial journey. Embrace the process, celebrate your progress, and keep pushing forward!

Key Takeaways

1. Set SMART Goals: Establish specific, measurable, achievable, relevant, and time-bound financial goals to create a clear roadmap for your financial journey.

2. Break It Down: Divide larger goals into manageable milestones, allowing for easier tracking of progress and keeping motivation high as you celebrate small victories.

3. Align with Values: Ensure your financial goals reflect your personal or business values, fostering a sense of purpose and commitment to achieving them.

4. Regularly Review and Adjust: Periodically assess your progress towards your goals and be flexible enough to adjust them as needed based on changing circumstances or priorities.

5. Stay Accountable: Share your financial goals with a trusted friend or mentor to enhance accountability and gain support on your path to financial success.

Conclusion

In the journey toward financial success, defining clear financial goals and milestones is your roadmap, guiding you through the complexities of wealth accumulation. By adopting the SMART framework—specific, measurable, achievable, relevant, and time-bound—you transform vague aspirations into concrete targets. Just as a compass directs a traveller, your milestones help you track progress and stay aligned with your long-term objectives. Remember, as you pursue your financial ambitions, "Success is the sum of small efforts, repeated day in and day out." By committing to this structured approach, you not only pave the way for personal and business growth but also cultivate the discipline needed to navigate the ever-changing landscape of financial opportunities.

Chapter 2: Developing a Strategic Plan for Wealth Accumulation

Introduction

In today's fast-paced financial landscape, mastering the art of wealth accumulation is essential for individuals and businesses alike. This chapter serves as your roadmap to financial growth, guiding you through the essential components of a robust strategic plan. We'll begin by helping you assess your current financial status, giving you a clear picture of where you stand. From there, we'll identify potential income sources that can fuel your growth, followed by a step-by-step approach to creating a tailored plan that encompasses smart savings, savvy investments, and effective asset management. By the end of this chapter, you'll have the tools and knowledge needed to confidently embark on your journey toward financial prosperity.

Strategic Wealth Accumulation Guide for Financial Growth

Wealth accumulation is a journey that requires careful planning, strategic thinking, and disciplined execution. Whether you're an individual looking to boost your finances or a business aiming for growth, understanding the fundamentals of wealth accumulation is essential. In this guide, we will explore key components of a comprehensive strategy, including assessing your current financial status, identifying potential income sources, and formulating a robust plan that incorporates savings, investments, and asset management.

1. Assessing Your Current Financial Status

A) Understanding Your Financial Picture

Before you can build wealth, you need to know where you currently stand. Start by creating a detailed inventory of your finances:

i) Net Worth Calculation: Subtract your total liabilities from your total assets. This figure gives you a snapshot of your financial health. For example, if your assets (home, savings, investments) total $300,000 and your liabilities (loans, credit card debt) total $100,000, your net worth is $200,000.

ii) Income vs. Expenses: Track your monthly income against your expenses. Use tools like spreadsheets or budgeting apps to categorize your spending. This will help you identify areas where you can cut back or save more.

B) Benefits of a Financial Assessment

a) Clarity: Understanding your financial status clarifies your strengths and weaknesses, guiding your strategy.

b) Motivation: Seeing your financial position can inspire you to set and achieve specific goals.

c) Tailored Strategies: A thorough assessment allows you to create a customized plan that addresses your unique circumstances.

2. Identifying Potential Income Sources

A) Exploring Diverse Income Streams

To accumulate wealth effectively, consider diversifying your income sources. Relying solely on one source can be risky. Here are some potential avenues:

i) Side Hustles: Identify skills or passions you can monetize. For instance, freelance graphic design, tutoring, or e-commerce can generate extra income.

ii) Passive Income: Explore options like rental properties, dividend-paying stocks, or peer-to-peer lending. These avenues can provide income with minimal ongoing effort.

iii) Investments: Invest in stocks, bonds, mutual funds, or ETFs. Research and understand the risks and returns associated with different asset classes.

B) Benefits of Multiple Income Sources

i) Financial Security: Multiple income streams reduce dependency on a single pay check, providing a buffer against economic downturns.

ii) Accelerated Growth: Diverse sources can enhance your overall income, allowing you to save and invest more effectively.

3. Formulating a Comprehensive Plan

A) Savings Strategy

Building a robust savings strategy is crucial for wealth accumulation. Here's how to get started:

i) Emergency Fund: Aim to save 3-6 months' worth of living expenses in a high-yield savings account. This fund acts as a financial cushion against unexpected expenses.

ii) Savings Goals: Set clear goals, such as saving for a home, education, or retirement. Use the SMART criteria (Specific, Measurable, Achievable, Relevant, Time-bound) to define these goals.

B) Investment Strategy

Investing is a powerful tool for wealth accumulation. Here are essential components to consider:

- Risk Assessment: Understand your risk tolerance—are you conservative, moderate, or aggressive? This will guide your investment choices.

- Asset Allocation: Diversify your investments across different asset classes to mitigate risk. A typical allocation might be 60% stocks, 30% bonds, and 10% cash.

- Regular Contributions: Consider dollar-cost averaging, where you invest a fixed amount regularly, reducing the impact of market volatility.

C) Asset Management Strategy

Effective asset management is key to maximizing your returns:

- Review and Rebalance: Regularly review your investment portfolio to ensure it aligns with your goals. Rebalance as necessary to maintain your desired asset allocation.

- Tax Efficiency: Be mindful of taxes when investing. Utilize tax-advantaged accounts like IRAs or 401(k)s to enhance your savings.

4. Monitoring and Adjusting Your Plan

A) The Importance of Regular Reviews

Wealth accumulation is not a one-time effort; it requires ongoing monitoring and adjustments:

- Track Progress: Set quarterly or annual reviews to assess whether you are on track to meet your financial goals. Use financial software or apps for easy tracking.

- Adapt to Changes: Life circumstances can change—job loss, market fluctuations, or unexpected expenses. Be prepared to adjust your strategy accordingly.

B) Benefits of Continuous Monitoring

- Stay on Target: Regular reviews help ensure you remain focused on your goals.

- Enhanced Knowledge: Keeping abreast of your financial situation increases your financial literacy and confidence.

Summary

Wealth accumulation is a dynamic process that requires commitment, adaptability, and informed decision-making. By assessing your financial status, identifying diverse income sources, and implementing a comprehensive savings and investment strategy, you can set the stage for long-term financial success. Remember, the journey to financial security is a marathon, not a sprint. Stay disciplined, stay informed, and watch your wealth grow.

Observations

- Assess Your Financial Status: Understanding your current situation is foundational to your wealth-building journey.

- Diversify Income Streams: Explore various avenues for income to enhance security and growth potential.

- Create a Comprehensive Plan: Incorporate savings, investment, and asset management strategies tailored to your goals.

- Monitor and Adjust Regularly: Stay engaged with your finances, adapting your strategies as needed to ensure success.

By following these guidelines, you can master the money game and build a secure financial future for yourself or your business.

Key Takeaways

1. Assess Your Financial Foundation: Begin by thoroughly evaluating your current financial status to understand your assets, liabilities, and overall cash flow, which sets the stage for informed decision-making.

2. Diversify Income Streams: Explore and identify various potential income sources, such as side hustles, investments, or business ventures, to create a robust financial portfolio that mitigates risk and enhances stability.

3. Establish Clear Savings Goals: Set specific and achievable savings goals that align with your financial aspirations,

ensuring that a portion of your income consistently contributes to building your wealth.

4. Invest Wisely for Growth: Formulate a strategic investment plan that balances risk and reward, focusing on assets that have the potential for long-term appreciation and align with your overall financial objectives.

5. Implement Effective Asset Management: Regularly review and adjust your asset management strategies to optimize returns, ensuring that your financial resources are working efficiently towards your wealth accumulation goals.

Conclusion

To successfully navigate the journey of wealth accumulation, whether as an individual looking to enhance your financial standing or a business striving for growth, it's crucial to start with a clear understanding of your current financial landscape. Assessing where you stand today lays the foundation for identifying diverse income streams and potential opportunities. Next, craft a strategic plan that integrates smart savings habits, diversified investments, and effective asset management. As the saying goes, "Wealth isn't just about having money; it's about having options." By embracing a holistic approach that considers all facets of your financial life, you can unlock a future filled with possibility and prosperity. Remember, the road to wealth is paved with informed choices and consistent action.

Chapter 3: Monitoring Progress and Adjusting Strategies

Introduction

In the journey toward financial success, staying on course requires more than just setting goals; it demands a commitment to ongoing evaluation and adaptation. This chapter delves into the vital practice of monitoring your financial progress and adjusting your strategies as needed. By regularly assessing your financial plans and investment portfolios, you can identify what's working, what's not, and how to pivot in response to life's inevitable changes. Whether you're an individual looking to enhance your wealth or a business striving for growth, mastering the art of performance tracking will empower you to make informed decisions, seize new opportunities, and navigate challenges with confidence. Let's explore the tools and techniques that will help you stay agile and aligned with your financial aspirations.

Navigating Financial Growth

In the journey of financial growth, whether for an individual or a business, the importance of regular assessment cannot be overstated. Just as a ship must adjust its sails to navigate changing winds, so too must your financial strategies evolve in response to new information, market trends, and personal circumstances. In this discussion, we will examine the critical components of monitoring progress and adjusting strategies. We aim to provide actionable insights that empower you to stay on course toward achieving your financial goals.

The Importance of Regular Assessments

A) Why Monitor Progress?

Regular assessments are essential for several reasons:

1. Stay Aligned with Goals: Financial goals can shift due to changes in personal circumstances, market conditions, or life stages. Periodic reviews help ensure that your strategies remain aligned with your evolving objectives.

2. Identify Opportunities and Risks: The financial landscape is dynamic. By regularly analyzing your portfolio, you can uncover new opportunities for growth or recognize emerging risks before they become significant issues.

3. Enhance Decision-Making: Informed adjustments lead to smarter financial decisions. Monitoring performance equips you with the data needed to make confident, strategic moves.

B) Key Techniques for Tracking Performance

1. Establish Clear Metrics

Start by defining what success looks like for you. Common metrics include:

- Return on Investment (ROI): Measures the profitability of an investment relative to its cost.

- Net Worth: The difference between assets and liabilities, providing a snapshot of overall financial health.

- Cash Flow: Tracking income versus expenses to ensure liquidity.

Example: If you invest in stocks, regularly assess the ROI to determine if they are performing as expected compared to benchmarks like the S&P 500.

2. Use Financial Tools

Leverage technology to simplify the tracking process. Tools like budgeting apps, investment platforms, and financial dashboards can provide real-time insights.

- Benefits: Automation reduces manual errors, saves time, and offers a comprehensive view of your finances.

- Example: A budgeting app can help you visualize spending patterns, making it easier to identify areas for cutbacks or reallocations.

3. Schedule Regular Reviews

Set a calendar reminder for quarterly or bi-annual reviews. Consistency is key.

- Benefits: Regular reviews create a habit of mindfulness around your finances, making it easier to catch potential issues early.

- Example: During your review, compare your investment performance against your initial goals. If you're consistently underperforming, it might be time to consider rebalancing.

C) Making Informed Adjustments

1. Analyze Performance Data

Once you have your metrics in place, dig into the data:

- Identify Trends: Look for patterns over time. Are certain investments consistently performing better?

- Evaluate Against Benchmarks: Compare your performance to industry standards to gauge your success.

Crucial Finding: Many investors fail to realize that not all investments will perform equally. Diversification can help mitigate risks while capitalizing on stronger performers.

2. Reassess Your Risk Tolerance

As life circumstances change—such as career advancements, family changes, or market volatility—your risk tolerance may shift.

- Example: If you recently received a promotion with a significant pay increase, you might feel more comfortable taking on higher-risk investments.

3. Adapt Your Strategy

Based on your analysis, be prepared to adjust your strategy:

- Rebalance Your Portfolio: If one investment has outperformed and now makes up too large a percentage of your portfolio, consider selling a portion and reallocating to under represented assets.

- Explore New Opportunities: Stay informed about emerging markets or innovative investment products that align with your goals.

4. Document Changes

Keep a record of your assessments and the adjustments made. This practice not only helps in tracking your financial journey but also provides valuable insights for future decision-making.

Summary

Monitoring progress and adjusting strategies is not merely a best practice; it's a fundamental aspect of financial growth. By establishing clear metrics, utilizing effective tools, and committing to regular assessments, you position yourself to navigate the complexities of financial planning with confidence. Remember, the financial landscape is ever-changing, and your strategies should reflect that dynamism. Embrace the process, stay informed, and watch your wealth accumulate over time.

Key Takeaways

1. Regular Assessments Are Essential: Consistently evaluate your financial plans and investment portfolios to ensure alignment with your evolving goals and market conditions.

2. Use Clear Metrics for Tracking: Establish specific, measurable criteria to assess performance, allowing you to easily identify areas for improvement or adjustment.

3. Stay Informed on Market Trends: Keep abreast of economic changes and industry developments, enabling you to make informed decisions about necessary strategy tweaks.

4. Embrace Flexibility in Your Approach: Be prepared to adapt your strategies as circumstances change, ensuring your financial plan remains relevant and effective.

5. Seek Professional Guidance When Needed: Don't hesitate to consult financial experts to gain insights and support for optimizing your growth strategies and overcoming challenges.

Conclusion

In the journey of wealth accumulation, monitoring progress and adjusting strategies is like steering a ship through changing tides; regular assessments of your financial plans and investment portfolios ensure you stay on course toward your goals. Embrace tools like budgeting apps and performance trackers to gain insights into your financial health, allowing you to pivot and adapt as life unfolds. Remember, "Success is a series of small wins," so celebrate your progress, learn from setbacks, and refine your approach. By staying proactive and flexible, you'll not only enhance your financial resilience but also create a dynamic roadmap to prosperity that evolves with you.

Chapter 4: Understanding Basic Financial Concepts

Introduction

In the journey to financial mastery, understanding basic financial concepts is like having a map before setting off on an adventure; it guides you through the twists and turns of budgeting, investing, and wealth accumulation. This chapter serves as your essential primer, breaking down complex ideas into simple, actionable steps. You'll discover how to create a budget that empowers your spending, explore various investing strategies to grow your wealth, and uncover the magic of compound interest, which can turn even modest savings into significant assets over time. With this foundational knowledge, you'll be well-equipped to navigate your financial future with confidence and clarity.

Secrets to Smart Money Management

In the journey to financial well-being, grasping basic financial concepts is crucial. This discussion serves as a primer, establishing the foundation for effective money management—whether you're an individual looking to enhance your personal finances or a business aiming for growth. By breaking down essential ideas like budgeting, investing strategies, and compound interest, we aim to empower you with the knowledge to make informed decisions.

1. Budgeting: The Foundation of Financial Management

A) What is Budgeting?

Budgeting is the process of creating a plan to manage your income and expenses. It acts as a financial roadmap, helping you navigate your financial landscape effectively.

B) Effective Strategies for Budgeting

- The 50/30/20 Rule: Allocate 50% of your income to needs (housing, food), 30% to wants (entertainment, travel), and 20% to savings and debt repayment. This simple guideline ensures a balanced approach to spending and saving.

- Track Your Expenses: Use apps or spreadsheets to monitor where your money goes. This visibility helps identify unnecessary expenditures, enabling you to adjust your budget accordingly.

- Set Specific Goals: Establish clear financial goals, like saving for a vacation or a new car. Having targets makes it easier to stay committed to your budget.

C) Benefits of Budgeting

- Financial Awareness: Knowing your spending habits allows for better decision-making and prioritization.

- Debt Management: A solid budget helps in identifying and reducing debt by allocating funds specifically for repayment.

- Emergency Preparedness: By budgeting for savings, you build a safety net for unexpected expenses, reducing financial stress.

D) Example

Imagine you earn $3,000 a month. Following the 50/30/20 rule, you would allocate $1,500 to needs, $900 to wants, and $600 to savings. By adhering to this structure, you ensure that all areas of your finances are accounted for, fostering financial health.

2. Investing Strategies: Growing Your Wealth

A) Understanding Investing

Investing is the process of allocating resources, usually money, to generate income or profit. Unlike saving, which typically involves low-risk accounts, investing carries a higher risk but also offers the potential for greater rewards.

B) Effective Investing Strategies

- Diversification: Spread your investments across various asset classes (stocks, bonds, real estate) to mitigate risk. This strategy helps protect your portfolio against market volatility.

- Dollar-Cost Averaging: Invest a fixed amount regularly, regardless of market conditions. This approach reduces the impact of market fluctuations and lowers the average cost per share over time.

- Long-Term Focus: Avoid the temptation to react to short-term market movements. Investing with a long-term perspective can yield substantial growth, especially through compound interest.

C) Benefits of Investing

- Wealth Accumulation: Investing allows your money to work for you, potentially yielding higher returns compared to traditional savings accounts.

- Inflation Hedge: Over time, investments can outpace inflation, preserving and growing your purchasing power.

- Passive Income: Certain investments, like dividends from stocks or rental income from properties, provide ongoing income streams.

D) Example

Consider investing $5,000 in a diversified portfolio with an average annual return of 7%. After 30 years, that investment could grow to over $38,000, illustrating the power of long-term investing and compound interest.

3. The Principle of Compound Interest: Your Money's Best Friend

A) What is Compound Interest?

Compound interest is the interest calculated on the initial principal and also on the accumulated interest from previous periods. This exponential growth is a powerful tool for wealth accumulation.

B) Effective Strategies to Utilize Compound Interest

- Start Early: The earlier you begin investing, the more time your money has to grow. Even small contributions can lead to significant gains over time due to compounding.

- Reinvest Earnings: Instead of cashing out dividends or interest payments, reinvest them to accelerate growth. This strategy amplifies the effects of compounding.

- **Consistent Contributions:** Regularly contribute to your investments or savings. This consistency not only boosts your initial investment but also enhances the compounding effect.

C) Benefits of Compound Interest

- **Exponential Growth:** Compound interest enables your wealth to grow at an increasing rate, creating a snowball effect over time.

- **Financial Freedom:** With effective compounding, you can achieve your financial goals sooner, enabling earlier retirement or the ability to pursue passions.

D) Example

If you invest $1,000 at an annual interest rate of 5%, compounding annually, after 20 years, you would have approximately $2,653. This demonstrates how starting early and allowing your investment to grow can lead to substantial financial rewards.

Summary

Understanding and applying these basic financial concepts—budgeting, investing strategies, and compound interest—forms the cornerstone of effective financial management. By mastering these principles, individuals and businesses can navigate their financial journeys with confidence, ultimately leading to increased wealth and security. As you implement these strategies, remember that patience and consistency are key; the journey to financial success is a marathon, not a sprint.

Key Takeaways

1. Budgeting Basics: Creating a clear budget helps you track income and expenses, enabling you to allocate funds effectively and save for your financial goals.

2. Investing Wisely: Diversifying your investments across different asset classes reduces risk and increases the potential for returns, ensuring your money grows over time.

3. Understanding Compound Interest: The power of compound interest means that your earnings generate their own earnings, making it crucial to start investing early to maximize your wealth.

4. Emergency Fund Importance: Building an emergency fund with three to six months' worth of expenses protects you from unexpected financial setbacks and provides peace of mind.

5. Financial Goals Setting: Clearly defining short-term and long-term financial goals gives you direction and motivation, allowing you to measure your progress and adjust your strategies as needed.

Conclusion

To thrive in the financial landscape, it's essential to master the basics—budgeting, investing, and the magic of compound interest. Think of your finances like a garden: budgeting is the careful planting of seeds, investing is nurturing those seeds to grow, and compound interest is the sunlight that accelerates their growth over time. By understanding these core concepts, you not only build a solid foundation for personal wealth or business expansion but also empower yourself to make informed decisions that pave the way for lasting success. Remember, "It's not about how much you make, but how much you keep and grow."

Embrace these strategies, and you'll be well on your way to mastering your money game.

Chapter 5: Staying Updated on Market Trends

Introduction

In today's fast-paced financial landscape, staying informed about market trends is essential for anyone looking to boost their finances or grow a business. This chapter delves into the significance of understanding both global and local economic shifts, breaking down complex market indicators into simple concepts that anyone can grasp. By mastering these insights, you can make informed decisions that not only safeguard your financial future but also position you to seize opportunities as they arise. Whether you're an individual aiming to enhance your savings or a business leader strategizing for growth, this knowledge will empower you to navigate the ever-changing market with confidence and clarity.

Understanding Market Trends

In today's fast-paced financial landscape, staying updated on market trends is crucial for both individuals looking to enhance their finances and businesses aiming for growth. Market trends encompass a wide array of factors, including economic indicators, consumer behaviour, and geopolitical events. By understanding these trends, you can make informed decisions that positively impact your financial health.

Importance of Market Awareness

1. Informed Decision-Making: Staying updated allows you to make decisions based on current data rather than assumptions. For individuals, this could mean knowing when to invest or save. For businesses, it might involve adjusting product offerings based on consumer demand.

Example: If a tech entrepreneur recognizes a rising trend in remote work technologies, they might pivot their product development to include features that cater specifically to remote teams.

2. Risk Management: Awareness of market trends can help mitigate financial risks. Understanding potential downturns can prompt pre-emptive measures to safeguard your investments or business operations.

Example: A small retail business noticing a trend towards online shopping can invest in e-commerce solutions before losing customers to competitors who have already made the shift.

Analyzing Complex Market Indicators

Market indicators, such as unemployment rates, inflation, and consumer confidence indices, provide valuable insights into the health of the economy. Learning to analyze these indicators can be the difference between thriving and merely surviving in a fluctuating market.

1. Economic Indicators: These include metrics like GDP growth, interest rates, and inflation. For individuals, knowing how these affect personal borrowing costs and investment returns is vital.

For businesses, these indicators can signal when to expand or scale back.

Crucial Finding: A rise in interest rates often leads to decreased consumer spending, which can negatively impact sales for businesses relying on discretionary purchases.

2. Consumer Behaviour Trends: Understanding shifts in consumer preferences can inform marketing strategies and product development. Tools such as social media analytics, surveys, and sales data can help businesses gauge what customers want.

Observation: A surge in sustainability awareness may prompt businesses to adopt eco-friendly practices, attracting a growing demographic of conscious consumers.

Effective Strategies for Staying Informed

1. Continuous Learning: Engage in ongoing education through financial news, economic reports, and online courses. Platforms like Coursera or LinkedIn Learning offer valuable resources.

Example: A business owner could enrol in a course on digital marketing trends to better reach an audience increasingly driven by online content.

2. Networking and Collaboration: Join industry groups, attend conferences, and connect with like-minded professionals. This not only keeps you updated but also opens doors to collaboration and innovation.

Benefit: Networking can lead to partnerships that provide shared insights into market trends, enhancing both parties' strategic approaches.

3. Utilize Technology: Leverage financial apps and market analysis tools to track trends in real-time. Many platforms offer customizable alerts for specific economic indicators.

Example: An individual investor might use a stock trading app that sends notifications when major economic reports are released, allowing them to react swiftly.

Summary

Staying updated on market trends is not just beneficial; it is essential for anyone looking to boost their financial situation or grow their business. By understanding economic indicators, consumer behaviour, and leveraging technology and education, you can position yourself ahead of the curve. In a world where change is the only constant, being informed is your best strategy for sustainable financial success. Whether you're an individual investor or a business owner, the proactive approach of monitoring market trends will empower you to make sound decisions that pave the way for a prosperous future.

Key Takeaways

1. Embrace Continuous Learning: Regularly educate yourself about economic shifts and market indicators to make informed financial decisions.

2. Analyze Local and Global Trends: Understand how both local and global economic conditions influence your financial landscape, enabling better strategic planning.

3. Utilize Technology and Tools: Leverage financial apps and analytical tools to track market changes and assess their potential impact on your finances.

4. Network with Financial Experts: Build relationships with industry professionals who can provide insights and guidance on navigating market fluctuations.

5. Adapt and Innovate: Stay flexible and ready to adjust your strategies based on evolving market conditions to maximize growth opportunities for your finances or business.

Conclusion

Staying updated on market trends is essential for anyone looking to boost their finances or grow their business. By closely monitoring global and local economic indicators, you can make informed decisions that align with current market conditions. For instance, understanding shifts in consumer behaviour or economic policies can help you adapt your strategies effectively. Remember, "Knowledge is the new currency"; the more you know, the better equipped you are to navigate challenges and seize opportunities. By embracing continuous learning and remaining agile, you'll position yourself to thrive, whether you're an individual seeking financial stability or a business striving for growth. Stay curious, stay informed, and watch your wealth flourish!

Chapter 6: Identifying Market Gaps and Opportunities

Introduction

In today's ever-evolving marketplace, identifying gaps and unmet needs is crucial for anyone looking to boost their finances or drive business growth. This chapter will guide you through the essential steps of conducting effective market research, helping you uncover valuable insights into consumer behaviour and preferences. By understanding what your audience truly desires and where existing products fall short, you can unlock innovative opportunities for development that not only meet these needs but also position you ahead of the competition. Whether you're an aspiring entrepreneur or a seasoned business owner, mastering the art of spotting market gaps can transform your ideas into successful, profit-generating ventures.

Seizing Opportunity: Mastering Market Gaps for Financial Growth

In today's dynamic economic landscape, both individuals looking to enhance their financial situation and businesses striving for growth must become adept at identifying market gaps and opportunities. This not only requires a keen understanding of market dynamics but also a proactive approach to market research. Below, we explore effective strategies, examples, and benefits to help you master the art of recognizing and capitalizing on unmet needs in the market.

1. Understanding Market Research

A) Definition and Importance

Market research is the systematic process of gathering, analyzing, and interpreting information about a market, including information about the target audience, competitors, and the industry as a whole. It is essential for making informed decisions that lead to successful product development and business growth.

B) Benefits:

- Informed Decisions: Reduces risk by providing data-driven insights.
- Customer Insights: Enhances understanding of consumer needs and preferences.
- Competitive Advantage: Identifies what competitors are doing and where you can outperform them.

2. Analyzing Consumer Behaviour

A) Strategies for Understanding Consumers

To effectively identify market gaps, you must first understand consumer behaviour. Here are some strategies to achieve this:

- Surveys and Questionnaires: Collect qualitative and quantitative data directly from potential customers. Ask open-ended questions to gauge preferences and pain points.

Example: A new skincare brand could survey consumers about their biggest skin concerns and the types of products they currently use.

- Focus Groups: Engage a small group of target customers in discussions about their experiences, needs, and product expectations. This method allows for deeper insights into consumer psychology.

Example: A tech startup might gather a focus group to discuss features they desire in a new gadget.

- Social Media Listening: Monitor social media platforms to see what consumers are saying about your industry or products. Use tools to track relevant hashtags and keywords.

Example: A fashion retailer can identify trends and unmet needs by analyzing social media conversations around sustainability in fashion.

3. Identifying Gaps in the Market

A) Key Steps to Identify Gaps

Once you understand consumer behaviour, the next step is identifying gaps in the market. Here's how:

- SWOT Analysis: Conduct a SWOT (Strengths, Weaknesses, Opportunities, Threats) analysis to evaluate your current market position and identify potential gaps.

Example: A local café might realize that while there are many coffee shops, few offer vegan or gluten-free options, indicating an opportunity to cater to health-conscious consumers.

- Trend Analysis: Keep an eye on emerging trends in your industry. Use tools like Google Trends or industry reports to stay updated.

Example: An increasing demand for plant-based diets can indicate a gap for innovative plant-based food products.

- Competitor Analysis: Analyze competitors to find areas where they are underperforming or where customers express dissatisfaction.

Example: If a competitor's customer reviews frequently mention poor customer service, there's an opportunity to differentiate your business by prioritizing exceptional customer care.

4. Developing Innovative Products

A) From Idea to Execution

Identifying a gap is just the beginning. Transforming that insight into a successful product requires careful planning and execution:

- Prototype Development: Create a minimum viable product (MVP) to test your idea in the market. This allows for early feedback without heavy investment.

Example: A startup might develop a simple version of a new app and release it to a small audience to gather feedback.

- Iterative Testing: Use feedback from initial users to refine your product. Continuous improvement based on real user experiences is vital.

Example: A fitness app can implement user suggestions for features, making it more appealing based on direct user feedback.

5. Marketing Your Innovations

A) Strategies for Effective Marketing

Once you have a product ready to launch, effective marketing is crucial to ensure it reaches the right audience:

- Content Marketing: Create valuable content that addresses consumer pain points and highlights how your product solves these issues.

Example: A company selling eco-friendly cleaning products could publish articles on the environmental impact of traditional cleaning agents.

- Social Media Campaigns: Utilize targeted ads on social media platforms to reach your desired audience, emphasizing your unique selling proposition.

Example: Launch a campaign showcasing user testimonials and before-and-after scenarios of using your product.

- Influencer Partnerships: Collaborate with influencers in your niche who resonate with your target audience to expand your reach.

Example: A health food brand could partner with fitness influencers to promote their new snack line.

Summary

Mastering the money game through effective market research and gap identification is essential for anyone looking to boost their finances or grow a business. By understanding consumer behaviour, identifying unmet needs, developing innovative products, and executing strategic marketing campaigns, you can position yourself for success in an ever-evolving market. Remember, the key is to remain agile, listen to your audience, and continuously adapt to their changing needs. Embrace these strategies, and watch your financial and business growth flourish.

Key Takeaways

1. Know Your Audience: Conduct thorough research to understand consumer preferences and pain points, ensuring your products or services resonate with their needs.

2. Analyze Trends: Stay updated on industry trends and shifts in consumer behaviour to spot emerging opportunities and adapt your strategies accordingly.

3. Leverage Data: Use quantitative and qualitative data analysis to identify gaps in the market, enabling you to create innovative solutions that fulfill unmet demands.

4. Test and Iterate: Develop prototypes and conduct market tests to gather feedback, allowing you to refine your offerings based on real customer insights.

5. Collaborate and Network: Engage with industry experts and potential customers to uncover hidden opportunities and gain diverse perspectives on market needs.

Conclusion

Mastering the money game requires a keen ability to identify market gaps and seize opportunities that others may overlook. By conducting thorough market research and analyzing consumer behaviour, you can uncover unmet needs that pave the way for innovative product development. Remember, as Peter Drucker said, "The best way to predict the future is to create it." Embracing this mindset allows you to transform insights into actionable solutions that resonate with your audience, ultimately turning knowledge into profit. Whether you're an individual aiming to enhance your financial standing or a business striving for growth, staying attuned to the evolving marketplace and remaining adaptable will empower you to not just survive but thrive in today's competitive landscape.

Chapter 7: Developing Innovative Products and Services

Introduction

In today's fast-paced economy, the key to financial success lies not just in managing what you have, but in innovating for the future. In this chapter, we delve into the exciting world of developing innovative products and services, where your ideas can transform into profitable ventures. We'll guide you through the essential steps of identifying market needs, brainstorming creative solutions, and crafting prototypes that resonate with customers. By embracing a cycle of continuous improvement through customer feedback, you can refine your offerings and ensure they not only meet demand but also stand out in a crowded marketplace. Let's unlock the potential for growth and financial freedom through innovative thinking!

Blueprint to Wealth: Strategies for Financial Success

In the quest for financial growth, whether for individuals or businesses, understanding and implementing effective wealth accumulation strategies is essential. This guide delves into key principles and strategies that can pave the way to financial success, emphasizing the importance of identifying market demands, ideation, prototyping, and utilizing customer feedback.

1. Understanding Market Demands

Strategy: Market Research

Before diving into wealth accumulation, it's crucial to understand the market landscape. Conduct thorough research to identify trends, gaps, and customer needs.

Example: A startup noticed a rising demand for eco-friendly products. By surveying potential customers, they discovered a preference for sustainable packaging, guiding their product development.

Benefits:

- Informed decision-making
- Reduced risk of product failure
- Tailored offerings that resonate with consumers

2. Ideation: Generating Innovative Solutions

Strategy: Brainstorming Sessions

Gather a diverse team to brainstorm ideas for products or services that align with identified market demands. Encourage creativity and think outside the box.

Example: A tech company gathered engineers and marketers to generate ideas for a new app. They focused on features that enhance user experience and fulfill unaddressed needs.

Benefits:

- Diverse perspectives lead to more innovative ideas
- Fosters a culture of collaboration

- Increases engagement among team members

3. Prototyping: Bringing Ideas to Life

Strategy: Develop Minimum Viable Products (MVPs)

Create a simplified version of your product that includes only the essential features. This allows you to test the concept without significant investment.

Example: A fashion brand launched a limited line of clothing with unique designs to gauge market interest before expanding the collection.

Benefits:

- Quick validation of ideas
- Cost-effective testing before full-scale launch
- Ability to gather real user data

4. Customer Feedback: Refining Offerings

Strategy: Implement Feedback Loops

Once the MVP is launched, actively seek customer feedback to understand what works and what doesn't. This can be done through surveys, interviews, and usage analytics.

Example: A food delivery service analyzed customer ratings and feedback, discovering that users preferred quicker delivery times and more sustainable packaging options.

Benefits:

- Continuous improvement of products and services
- Builds customer loyalty through engagement

- Identifies new opportunities for enhancement

5. Scaling and Growth: Leveraging Success

Strategy: Invest in Marketing and Partnerships

Once a product is refined and meets market needs, invest in marketing to reach a broader audience. Explore partnerships that can enhance visibility and credibility.

Example: A local gym partnered with a wellness brand to offer joint promotions, attracting more customers to both businesses.

Benefits:

- Expands reach and brand awareness
- Increases sales through collaborative efforts
- Strengthens community ties and brand reputation

Crucial Findings and Observations

- **Continuous Adaptation is Key:** The market is ever-evolving. Regularly reassess your strategies and offerings to stay relevant.

- **Customer-Centric Approach Drives Success:** Businesses that prioritize customer needs are more likely to achieve sustainable growth.

- **Data is Your Ally:** Leverage data analytics to inform decisions and improve offerings.

- **Risk Management Matters:** Diversifying investments and products can mitigate risks associated with market fluctuations.

- Network and Collaborate: Building relationships within your industry can open doors to new opportunities and insights.

Summary

Mastering the money game is not merely about accumulating wealth; it's about understanding the dynamics of the market, innovating based on real needs, and continually refining your approach. By following these strategies, individuals and businesses alike can navigate the complexities of financial growth effectively, ensuring they not only meet market demands but also exceed them. Embrace innovation, seek feedback, and always be prepared to adapt; this is the pathway to enduring success in today's competitive landscape.

Key Takeaways

- Identify Your Goals: Clearly define your financial objectives, whether saving for retirement or expanding your business, as this sets a roadmap for your wealth-building journey.

- Budget Smartly: Create a realistic budget that tracks your income and expenses, allowing you to allocate funds effectively and identify areas for potential savings.

- Invest Wisely: Diversify your investments to minimize risk and maximize returns, focusing on opportunities that align with your financial goals and market trends.

- Embrace Continuous Learning: Stay informed about financial strategies and market developments to adapt and refine your approach, ensuring sustained growth and resilience.

- Leverage Customer Feedback: Use insights from your target audience to refine your products and services, enhancing their value and meeting market demands effectively.

Conclusion

Developing innovative products and services is crucial for enhancing financial performance and fostering business growth. By prioritizing the process of ideation, you can generate fresh ideas that meet real market demands. Prototyping allows you to test these concepts, while customer feedback acts as a critical tool for refinement, ensuring your offerings truly resonate with your target audience. This iterative process not only enhances product quality but also fosters a deeper connection with customers, paving the way for long-term success. As you embark on this journey, remember that each innovative solution is a strategic step toward accumulating wealth and achieving financial freedom.

Chapter 8: Leveraging Digital Platforms for Scalability

Introduction

In today's fast-paced digital landscape, leveraging online platforms isn't just an option; it's a game changer for anyone looking to boost their finances or scale their business. This chapter delves into the powerful role of digital tools in expanding your reach and enhancing your scalability. From social media and e-commerce to email marketing and analytics, we'll explore effective strategies that maximize your visibility and engagement in the bustling digital marketplace. Whether you're an aspiring entrepreneur or a seasoned business owner, understanding how to harness these platforms can unlock new opportunities for growth and financial success.

Digital Leverage: Unlocking Growth in a Fast-Paced World

In today's fast-paced world, businesses looking to grow must embrace digital platforms. These online tools are not just optional; they are essential for reaching new customers and maximizing engagement. In this chapter, we'll explore how to effectively use these platforms to expand your reach and achieve scalability.

Understanding Digital Platforms

Digital platforms encompass various online tools and environments where businesses can connect with customers, promote products, and engage audiences. This includes social media, e-commerce sites, websites, and email marketing. Each platform offers unique opportunities to enhance visibility and drive growth.

Benefits of Digital Platforms

1. Wider Audience Reach

Digital platforms allow businesses to reach potential customers beyond geographical limitations. A local store can become a global player overnight by establishing an online presence. For instance, using platforms like Facebook and Instagram enables businesses to target specific demographics, effectively tailoring marketing efforts.

2. Cost-Effective Marketing

Traditional advertising can be expensive, but digital marketing often offers more cost-effective alternatives. Tools like Google Ads or Facebook Ads allow businesses to set their budgets, track results, and optimize campaigns in real-time. This precision can yield higher returns on investment.

3. Enhanced Customer Engagement

Digital platforms facilitate direct interaction with customers. Businesses can gather feedback, answer questions, and create communities around their brand. Engaging content, such as polls, Q&A sessions, and live videos, can boost loyalty and foster a sense of belonging among customers.

4. Data-Driven Insights

One of the most significant advantages of digital platforms is the ability to collect and analyze data. This information can guide decision-making processes, helping businesses understand customer preferences and behaviours. Tools like Google Analytics provide insights into website traffic, allowing for continuous improvement of marketing strategies.

Effective Strategies for Maximizing Visibility

To fully leverage digital platforms, consider implementing the following strategies:

1. Create a Strong Online Presence

- Website Optimization

Your website is often the first point of contact for potential customers. Ensure it is user-friendly, mobile-responsive, and optimized for search engines (SEO). A well-structured website enhances visibility and improves user experience.

- Content Marketing

Develop valuable content that addresses the needs and interests of your target audience. Blog posts, videos, infographics, and podcasts can position your brand as an authority in your industry while driving organic traffic to your site.

2. Utilize Social Media Effectively

- Choose the Right Platforms

Identify which social media platforms your target audience frequents. Focus your efforts on those channels to ensure maximum engagement. For example, Instagram is ideal for visual content, while LinkedIn is better for B2B marketing.

- Engagement and Community Building

Foster relationships with your audience by responding to comments, sharing user-generated content, and hosting giveaways. Creating a community around your brand can enhance loyalty and encourage word-of-mouth referrals.

3. Implement Email Marketing

- Build an Email List

Collect email addresses through sign-up forms on your website or social media. Offer incentives such as discounts or exclusive content to encourage subscriptions.

- Personalized Campaigns

Segment your email list based on customer preferences and behaviours. Tailor your messaging to different segments to increase relevance and engagement. Personalized emails can lead to higher open and conversion rates.

4. Leverage E-Commerce Platforms

- Set Up Online Store fronts

Platforms like Shopify, Etsy, or Amazon allow businesses to sell products online with minimal setup. Invest time in creating appealing product listings and optimizing them for search engines.

- Streamline the Checkout Process

A complicated checkout process can lead to cart abandonment. Ensure your e-commerce site is easy to navigate, with a simple, secure payment process to enhance the customer experience.

5. Invest in Paid Advertising

- Targeted Advertising

Use pay-per-click (PPC) advertising to reach specific audiences based on demographics, interests, and behaviours. This approach can drive traffic quickly and generate leads.

- Retargeting Strategies

Implement retargeting ads to re-engage visitors who didn't convert during their first visit. These ads can serve as reminders of products or services, increasing the likelihood of conversion.

Examples of Successful Digital Scalability

1. Airbnb: By leveraging digital platforms, Airbnb transformed the travel industry. Their user-friendly website and mobile app connect hosts with travellers globally, creating a scalable model that continues to grow.

2. Dollar Shave Club: This subscription-based service used viral marketing strategies on social media to reach millions. Their humorous and relatable content not only built brand awareness but also fostered a loyal customer base.

3. Warby Parker: By utilizing an innovative e-commerce platform, Warby Parker disrupted the eyewear industry. Their try-at-home program combined with strong social media presence allowed them to scale rapidly while providing exceptional customer service.

Crucial Findings and Observations

- Adaptability is Key: The digital landscape is ever-evolving. Successful businesses are those that continually adapt to new trends, tools, and consumer behaviours.

- Consistency Matters: Maintaining a consistent brand voice and messaging across all digital platforms builds trust and recognition. This consistency is essential for long-term success.

- Measure and Optimize: Regularly review analytics to understand what strategies are working. Be willing to pivot and optimize campaigns based on performance data to maximize growth.

Summary

Leveraging digital platforms is not merely a strategy for growth; it's a necessity in today's marketplace. By understanding the benefits, implementing effective strategies, and learning from successful examples, businesses can enhance their visibility, engage customers, and achieve scalable growth. In this digital age, those who embrace change and leverage technology will thrive, while those who resist may struggle to survive. Embrace the digital revolution, and unlock the potential for unlimited growth!

Key Takeaways

1. Embrace Online Presence: Establishing a strong online presence through websites and social media is crucial for attracting a wider audience and enhancing brand visibility.

2. Utilize Digital Marketing Tools: Harness tools like SEO, email marketing, and social media ads to effectively reach potential customers and drive traffic to your business.

3. Engage with Your Audience: Building meaningful relationships with your audience through interactive

content and responsive communication fosters loyalty and boosts engagement.

4. Analyze and Adapt: Regularly tracking metrics and analyzing user behaviour allows you to refine your strategies and optimize performance for better results.

5. Leverage E-commerce Solutions: Implementing e-commerce platforms enables seamless transactions and expands your market reach, driving sales growth in the digital space.

Conclusion

In today's fast-paced digital landscape, leveraging online platforms is not just a choice but a necessity for individuals and businesses aiming to enhance their financial growth. By harnessing tools like social media, e-commerce sites, and digital marketing strategies, you can dramatically increase your visibility and engagement, reaching a broader audience than ever before. As the saying goes, "Adapt or perish," and in this realm, adaptability means embracing the digital revolution to drive scalability and profitability. Whether you're a budding entrepreneur or an individual looking to boost your finances, integrating these digital strategies can transform your approach, making your financial goals not just achievable, but inevitable. Remember, in the game of wealth accumulation, those who master the digital arena will ultimately lead the way.

Chapter 9: Diversifying Investments Across Asset Classes

Introduction

In the journey to financial prosperity, one of the most effective strategies is diversifying investments across various asset classes. This chapter delves into the essential practice of diversification, highlighting how spreading your investments across stocks, bonds, and real estate can safeguard your portfolio against unexpected market fluctuations. By understanding the unique characteristics of each asset class and employing thoughtful strategies to balance risk and return, both individuals and businesses can enhance their financial resilience and create a more stable path toward wealth accumulation. Join us as we explore the key principles of diversification that can empower you to make informed investment decisions and unlock greater financial growth.

Spread the Wealth: Mastering Diversification for Investment Success

In the world of investing, diversification is like a safety net that helps protect your portfolio from market fluctuations. Think of it as not putting all your eggs in one basket. By spreading your investments across various asset classes, you can reduce risk while maximizing potential returns. This discussion highlights the importance of diversification and presents effective strategies for building a balanced investment portfolio.

Understanding Asset Classes

1. Stocks

Stocks represent ownership in a company. When you buy shares, you invest in its growth potential. While stocks can provide substantial returns, they also come with high volatility. For instance, during market downturns, stock prices can plummet, impacting your overall wealth.

2. Bonds

Bonds are essentially loans you give to governments or corporations in exchange for regular interest payments plus the return of the bond's face value at maturity. They are generally considered safer than stocks, offering more stability. For example, U.S. Treasury bonds are seen as low-risk, making them an excellent option for conservative investors.

3. Real Estate

Investing in real estate can provide passive income and appreciation. Properties can yield rental income and appreciate over time, serving as a hedge against inflation. However, managing real estate requires time and effort, so it's essential to weigh the benefits against the responsibilities involved.

4. Commodities

Commodities like gold, oil, and agricultural products can act as a safeguard during economic uncertainty. They often move independently of stocks and bonds, making them a valuable addition to a diversified portfolio. For instance, gold has historically been a safe haven during market downturns.

5. Alternative Investments

This category includes private equity, hedge funds, and collectibles. While they can provide higher returns, they often come with higher risks and less liquidity. Therefore, understanding these investments is crucial before diving in.

Strategies for Diversifying Your Portfolio

1. Asset Allocation

Determine your risk tolerance and investment goals. A common strategy is the 60/40 rule, where 60% of your portfolio is in stocks and 40% in bonds. Adjusting this mix based on your comfort with risk can help you achieve a balanced portfolio.

2. Geographic Diversification

Don't just invest in domestic markets. Global diversification can reduce risk associated with any one economy. Consider investing in international stocks and bonds to gain exposure to emerging markets.

3. Sector Diversification

Within stocks, diversify across various sectors such as technology, healthcare, and consumer goods. For example, if tech stocks are underperforming, a well-diversified portfolio with investments in healthcare may help mitigate losses.

4. Rebalancing

Regularly review and adjust your portfolio to maintain your desired asset allocation. Market fluctuations can skew your original plan, so rebalancing ensures you stay aligned with your investment strategy.

5. Investing in Index Funds or ETFs

These funds allow you to invest in a broad range of assets without having to pick individual stocks. They typically have lower fees and provide instant diversification, making them an excellent choice for beginner investors.

Benefits of Diversification

1. Risk Management

By investing in various asset classes, you can cushion your portfolio against significant losses. If one asset class underperforms, others may still yield positive returns, balancing your overall performance.

2. Potential for Higher Returns

A well-diversified portfolio can enhance returns over time. While it may seem counter intuitive, holding a mix of high-risk and low-risk investments can yield more consistent growth.

3. Peace of Mind

Knowing that your investments are spread out can provide psychological comfort. Investors who diversify often experience less stress during market volatility, allowing them to make rational decisions rather than emotional ones.

Crucial Findings and Observations

- Historical Performance: Studies show that diversified portfolios have outperformed concentrated ones over the long term. A well-balanced approach can help you weather economic storms and seize opportunities.
- Market Cycles: Different asset classes perform well during various economic cycles. For instance, stocks may flourish

in a booming economy, while bonds may be more stable during recessions.

- Behavioural Insights: Investors often fall prey to the temptation of chasing trends. A diversified approach discourages this behaviour by encouraging a long-term perspective focused on steady growth.

Summary

Diversification is not just a strategy; it's a fundamental principle of investing. By understanding different asset classes and implementing a thoughtful diversification plan, you can enhance your financial stability and growth potential. Whether you're an individual investor looking to boost your finances or a business aiming for growth, adopting these principles will equip you to navigate the complexities of the financial world with confidence.

Key Takeaways

1. Balance Risk and Return: Diversifying your investments across stocks, bonds, and real estate can help mitigate risks while optimizing potential returns, ensuring a more stable financial future.

2. Asset Class Understanding: Each asset class behaves differently under various market conditions, so knowing how they interact can enhance your investment strategy and lead to smarter decisions.

3. Strategic Allocation: Regularly assessing and adjusting your portfolio's asset allocation based on your financial goals and risk tolerance can keep your investments aligned with your long-term objectives.

4. Embrace Market Cycles: Diversification allows you to take advantage of different market cycles, enabling some investments to perform well when others may falter, thus smoothing out overall portfolio performance.

5. Continuous Learning: Staying informed about market trends and new asset classes will empower you to adapt your investment strategy, fostering both growth and resilience in your financial journey.

Conclusion

In the journey to financial success, remember the age-old adage: "Don't put all your eggs in one basket." Diversifying investments across asset classes—such as stocks, bonds, and real estate—not only cushions your portfolio against market volatility but also maximizes your potential for growth. By strategically balancing risk and return, you create a resilient financial foundation that can weather economic storms while capitalizing on diverse opportunities. Embrace the power of diversification, and you'll not only safeguard your wealth but also pave the way for greater financial freedom and prosperity. As you master the money game, let this principle guide your strategy: varied paths lead to robust riches.

Chapter 10: Long-term Growth and Income Strategies

Introduction

In today's fast-paced financial landscape, achieving lasting wealth isn't just about quick wins; it's about cultivating a garden of growth that flourishes over time. In this chapter, we'll explore the art of sustainable wealth accumulation through effective long-term strategies. From the power of dividend investing that rewards you regularly, to the smart reinvestment of your earnings that can exponentially boost your financial garden, we'll delve into the vital role patience plays in your journey. By understanding and implementing these foundational concepts, both individuals and businesses can create a reliable income stream and build a legacy of prosperity that stands the test of time.

Path to Financial Prosperity

Achieving financial success requires a blend of strategy, patience, and informed decision-making. In this guide, we will explore effective strategies for both individuals looking to boost their finances and businesses aiming for sustainable growth. We'll dive into key concepts like dividend investing, reinvestment strategies, and the importance of a patient mindset in wealth accumulation.

Understanding Wealth Accumulation

Wealth accumulation is not just about earning money; it's about making smart decisions that allow your wealth to grow over time. This involves understanding your financial goals, the power of compound interest, and the strategies that can help you achieve long-term financial stability.

1. Dividend Investing

What It Is: Dividend investing involves purchasing stocks from companies that return a portion of their profits to shareholders in the form of dividends.

Benefits:

- Regular Income: Dividends provide a steady income stream, making them ideal for both individuals and businesses needing consistent cash flow.

- Reinvestment Opportunities: Many investors choose to reinvest dividends, purchasing more shares and increasing potential returns over time.

Example: Consider a company like Johnson & Johnson, which has a long history of paying dividends. By investing in such a company, an investor not only benefits from potential stock price appreciation but also enjoys regular dividend payments.

Crucial Observations:

- Not all dividends are created equal; look for companies with a history of increasing dividends, which indicates strong financial health and management commitment to returning value to shareholders.

2. Reinvestment Strategies

What It Is: Reinvestment involves taking the returns from investments—whether from dividends, interest, or capital gains—and putting them back into the investment portfolio to buy more assets.

Benefits:

- Compounding Returns: The more you reinvest, the greater your potential returns, thanks to compound interest. This can significantly accelerate wealth accumulation over time.

- Market Timing Neutrality: By regularly reinvesting, you can take advantage of dollar-cost averaging, which mitigates the risks of market volatility.

Example: If you invest $1,000 in a mutual fund that returns 8% annually, rather than cashing out your earnings, reinvesting them could lead to exponential growth. Over 20 years, that initial investment could grow substantially more than if you simply withdrew the earnings each year.

Crucial Findings:

- Starting to reinvest early can lead to wealth accumulation that outpaces inflation and enhances financial security.

3. The Importance of Patience

What It Is: Patience is the cornerstone of successful investing. Wealth accumulation is not typically an overnight success; it requires time and a long-term perspective.

Benefits:

- Long-Term Growth: Markets can fluctuate in the short term, but historical trends show that long-term investments tend to yield positive returns.

- Reduced Stress: Adopting a patient mindset reduces anxiety associated with market volatility, allowing investors to make rational, rather than emotional, decisions.

Example: Historical data from the stock market demonstrates that, despite numerous downturns, those who remained invested through the Great Depression, the Dot-Com bubble, and the 2008 financial crisis saw significant recoveries and gains over time.

Crucial Observations:

- Investors who panic and sell during downturns often miss out on subsequent recoveries, underscoring the importance of staying the course.

4. Building a Diverse Portfolio

What It Is: Diversification involves spreading investments across various asset classes, sectors, and geographical regions to mitigate risk.

Benefits:

- Risk Management: A diversified portfolio can reduce the impact of poor-performing assets on overall returns.
- Enhanced Returns: Different asset classes often perform differently under varying market conditions, providing more stable returns over time.

Example: A well-rounded portfolio might include stocks, bonds, real estate, and commodities. During market downturns, some sectors may decline while others remain stable or even appreciate, cushioning overall losses.

Crucial Findings:

- Regularly reviewing and rebalancing your portfolio ensures it aligns with your risk tolerance and investment goals.

Summary

In summary, mastering the money game requires a strategic approach to wealth accumulation. By focusing on dividend investing, embracing reinvestment strategies, exercising patience, and building a diversified portfolio, individuals and businesses can achieve sustainable growth and consistent income over time. Remember, the journey to financial success is a marathon, not a sprint—invest wisely, stay patient, and watch your wealth grow.

Key Takeaways

1. Embrace Dividend Investing: Prioritize stocks that pay dividends to create a steady income stream, allowing your investments to grow while providing regular cash flow.

2. Reinvest for Greater Returns: Utilize a reinvestment strategy by plowing dividends back into your investments to compound your wealth over time, amplifying your financial growth.

3. Cultivate Patience: Understand that wealth accumulation is a marathon, not a sprint; staying committed to your long-term strategy is crucial for achieving significant financial milestones.

4. Diversify Your Portfolio: Spread your investments across various sectors and asset classes to mitigate risks and enhance the potential for steady returns, ensuring resilience against market fluctuations.

5. Educate Yourself Continuously: Keep learning about market trends and investment strategies, as staying informed empowers you to make smarter financial decisions that align with your growth objectives.

Conclusion

To boost your finances or elevate your business, embrace the power of long-term growth and consistent income through strategic investments and a patient mindset. Consider dividend investing as a cornerstone of your strategy—like planting a tree that bears fruit year after year, reinvesting those dividends can significantly compound your wealth over time. Remember, "Wealth is not just about having money; it's about creating a legacy." By focusing on sustainable growth, you not only secure your financial future but also position yourself to weather economic storms. Stay disciplined, prioritize reinvestment, and trust the process; with time and dedication, your efforts will flourish into a thriving financial ecosystem.

Chapter 11: Upgrading with Technological Advancements

Introduction

In today's fast-paced financial landscape, staying ahead requires more than just traditional strategies; it demands a commitment to leveraging the latest technological advancements. This chapter will explore how individuals and businesses alike can transform their financial practices by adopting cutting-edge tools and systems that streamline operations and boost productivity. By embracing these innovations, you not only enhance your efficiency but also position yourself or your business to thrive in an increasingly competitive market. Join us as we delve into the process of evaluating and implementing these transformative technologies, ensuring you are equipped to master the money game and secure your financial future.

Unlocking Success: Embrace Innovation for Growth

In today's fast-paced world, whether you're an individual aiming to improve your finances or a business seeking growth, embracing the latest technologies is essential. This discussion explores the critical role of adopting innovative tools and systems in enhancing operational efficiency and gaining a competitive edge. By strategically evaluating and implementing these technologies, you can unlock new opportunities for success.

Understanding the Need for Technological Advancement

A) The Digital Landscape

The digital landscape is constantly evolving. From mobile banking apps that simplify personal finance to sophisticated software that streamlines business operations, technology can significantly influence your financial trajectory. For individuals, this means accessing better tools for budgeting, investing, and saving. For businesses, it translates to improved productivity, better customer engagement, and ultimately, higher profits.

B) The Competitive Edge

In a crowded marketplace, maintaining a competitive edge is vital. Companies that leverage technology can adapt to changes quickly, offering better services and products than their competitors. For individuals, staying informed about financial technology (fintech) solutions can lead to smarter investment choices and enhanced financial literacy.

Evaluating Technological Tools

A) Identify Your Needs

Before diving into new technologies, it's crucial to assess your specific needs. For individuals, this might involve identifying financial goals—like saving for retirement or buying a home. Businesses should analyze operational bottlenecks or customer service challenges.

B) Research and Compare Solutions

Once you've identified your needs, research various tools and platforms. For instance, if budgeting is a challenge, compare personal finance apps such as Mint, YNAB, or Pocket Guard. For businesses, explore project management tools like Trello or Asana to enhance team collaboration.

C) Cost vs. Benefit Analysis

Evaluate the costs associated with adopting new technologies against the potential benefits. This includes not only the financial investment but also the time required for training and implementation. For example, implementing a customer relationship management (CRM) system might require upfront costs but can lead to improved customer retention and increased sales.

Implementing New Technologies

A) Start Small

For both individuals and businesses, starting with smaller, manageable technology implementations can ease the transition. Individuals can begin by using a budgeting app to track expenses, while businesses might pilot a new software solution with one team before rolling it out company-wide.

B) Training and Support

Invest in training to ensure that everyone is comfortable using the new tools. This reduces frustration and increases the likelihood of successful adoption. For example, a business can host workshops to train employees on using a new inventory management system, while individuals can take online courses to better understand investment platforms.

C) Monitor Progress

After implementation, continuously monitor the effectiveness of the technology. Collect feedback to understand what works and what doesn't. If a budgeting app is helping you save more, that's a success. For businesses, tracking metrics such as productivity or customer satisfaction can highlight the impact of new tools.

Benefits of Technological Advancements

A) Enhanced Efficiency

One of the most significant benefits of adopting new technology is enhanced efficiency. Automation of repetitive tasks allows individuals to focus on strategic financial planning and businesses to streamline operations. For instance, automating invoicing can save time and reduce human error.

B) Improved Decision-Making

With access to real-time data and analytics, both individuals and businesses can make informed decisions. For example, investment apps provide insights into market trends, helping users to make timely investment choices. Businesses can analyze sales data to adjust marketing strategies proactively.

C) Increased Accessibility

Technological advancements also enhance accessibility. Individuals can manage their finances anytime, anywhere, thanks to mobile apps. Businesses can reach broader markets through e-commerce platforms, expanding their customer base beyond geographical limits.

Crucial Findings and Observations

A) The Importance of Staying Updated

Technology is not static; it evolves rapidly. Regularly updating your knowledge and skills is crucial to leveraging advancements effectively. Follow industry news, attend workshops, or participate in webinars to stay informed.

B) The Role of Cybersecurity

As you adopt new technologies, never underestimate the importance of cybersecurity. Protecting your financial information should be a top priority. Use secure passwords, enable two-factor authentication, and educate yourself about online security best practices.

C) Long-Term Vision

Finally, while immediate benefits are important, consider the long-term implications of your technological investments. A technology that enhances current efficiency should also align with your long-term financial goals.

Summary

Embracing technological advancements is no longer an option; it's a necessity for financial success. By evaluating, implementing, and continuously adapting to new tools, both individuals and businesses can enhance efficiency, make informed decisions, and stay competitive in an ever-evolving landscape. Remember, the goal is not just to keep up with technology but to leverage it strategically to achieve your financial aspirations.

Key Takeaways

1. Embrace Innovation: Adopting the latest technologies can significantly streamline your operations and reduce costs, allowing you to focus more on growth strategies.

2. Evaluate Needs: Before implementing new tools, carefully assess your business needs to ensure the technology you choose aligns with your goals and enhances productivity.

3. Stay Competitive: Regularly updating your technology stack is essential for staying ahead in a rapidly evolving market, ensuring you offer the best services or products.

4. Invest Wisely: Consider the long-term benefits and ROI of any new system or tool, as strategic investments in technology can lead to substantial financial gains over time.

5. Train Your Team: Providing adequate training for your staff on new technologies fosters a culture of adaptability and innovation, ultimately driving your business toward success.

Conclusion

In today's fast-paced financial landscape, embracing technological advancements isn't just an option; it's a necessity for anyone looking to boost their finances or propel their business growth. By evaluating and implementing the latest tools—whether it's automation software for personal budgeting or data analytics for market insights—individuals and businesses can streamline operations and make informed decisions that drive wealth accumulation. As the saying goes, "The best way to predict the future is to create it." By harnessing technology effectively, you can not only stay competitive but also unlock new avenues for financial success, transforming challenges into opportunities with every innovative step you take.

Chapter 12: Exploring Emerging Sectors

Introduction

In today's fast-paced world, staying ahead of the financial curve means looking beyond traditional investment avenues and diving into emerging sectors that promise significant growth. This chapter explores exciting opportunities in cutting-edge fields like artificial intelligence, blockchain technology, and renewable energy, where innovation is reshaping industries and creating new wealth potential. By understanding these dynamic sectors and the trends driving them, you can position yourself or your business for future success. Join us as we uncover the possibilities that lie within these transformative markets and empower you to make informed investment decisions that could lead to substantial financial gains.

Navigating Key Investment Strategies

In today's rapidly evolving financial landscape, the ability to identify and invest in emerging sectors is crucial for individuals and businesses aiming to boost their financial standing. This discussion explores three transformative sectors: artificial intelligence (AI), blockchain technology, and renewable energy. Each of these sectors presents unique opportunities for growth and wealth accumulation. Let's explore these areas, effective strategies for engagement, and the potential benefits they offer.

1. Artificial Intelligence (AI)

A) Overview

Artificial intelligence is reshaping industries by automating processes, enhancing decision-making, and improving customer experiences. This sector is not just a trend; it represents a fundamental shift in how businesses operate.

B) Investment Opportunities

- AI Startups: Consider investing in innovative startups that leverage AI to solve real-world problems. These companies often have high growth potential, and early investment can yield substantial returns.

- AI-Driven Tools: Businesses can adopt AI tools that enhance productivity and streamline operations. For example, utilizing AI for data analysis can lead to better decision-making and cost savings.

C) Strategies for Engagement

- Stay Informed: Follow industry trends and reports to understand emerging technologies and applications within AI.

- Networking: Attend conferences and workshops to connect with thought leaders and other investors in the AI space.

D) Benefits

Investing in AI can lead to increased efficiency and innovation in your own business or investment portfolio. The potential for high returns is coupled with the opportunity to be part of a groundbreaking technological evolution.

2. Blockchain Technology

A) Overview

Blockchain technology is revolutionizing how data is stored and transactions are conducted. By providing a decentralized and secure way to record information, blockchain is gaining traction in finance, supply chain management, and beyond.

B) Investment Opportunities

- Cryptocurrencies: Consider investing in established cryptocurrencies like Bitcoin and Ethereum or exploring altcoins with strong use cases.

- Blockchain Startups: Identify startups that are utilizing blockchain to improve transparency and efficiency in various sectors, from finance to healthcare.

C) Strategies for Engagement

- Education: Take courses or read literature on blockchain to fully grasp its implications and potential.

- Diversification: Spread investments across different blockchain applications to mitigate risks and enhance potential returns.

D) Benefits

Blockchain can enhance security, reduce fraud, and increase operational efficiencies. For businesses, adopting blockchain solutions can lead to improved trust and transparency with customers and partners.

3. Renewable Energy

A) Overview

As the world shifts toward sustainable practices, renewable energy sources such as solar, wind, and hydroelectric power are gaining prominence. This sector is not only vital for environmental preservation but also presents lucrative investment opportunities.

B) Investment Opportunities

- Green Stocks: Invest in companies specializing in renewable energy technologies, such as solar panel manufacturers or wind farm developers.

- Sustainable Projects: Engage in crowdfunding platforms that support renewable energy projects, allowing you to invest in specific initiatives.

C) Strategies for Engagement

- Government Incentives: Keep an eye on governmental policies promoting renewable energy, as these can provide additional investment opportunities.

- Community Involvement: Participate in local sustainability initiatives to gain first hand experience and insights into the renewable energy landscape.

D) Benefits

Investing in renewable energy not only aligns with global sustainability goals but also positions you to benefit from a sector expected to grow significantly in the coming years. The long-term financial gains can be complemented by positive social and environmental impacts.

Summary

Staying informed and agile in the face of technological advancements is essential for individuals and businesses looking to enhance their financial futures. By exploring sectors like artificial intelligence, blockchain, and renewable energy, investors can uncover unique opportunities that promise not only substantial financial returns but also contribute to a more sustainable and innovative world.

Key Takeaways

1. Embrace Innovation: Invest in cutting-edge sectors like artificial intelligence and blockchain, as these technologies are reshaping industries and presenting new wealth-building opportunities.

2. Stay Informed: Continuously educate yourself about emerging trends and innovations to identify potential investment opportunities that can lead to substantial growth.

3. Diversify Investments: Spread your investments across various emerging sectors, such as renewable energy, to mitigate risk while maximizing your potential for returns.

4. Network Strategically: Connect with industry experts and thought leaders in these sectors to gain insights and access to exclusive investment opportunities.

5. Long-Term Vision: Adopt a forward-thinking mindset that prioritizes sustainable growth and aligns your financial strategies with the future direction of technology and market demands.

Conclusion

In today's rapidly evolving financial landscape, the key to unlocking substantial growth lies in embracing innovation and seizing opportunities within emerging sectors like artificial intelligence, blockchain, and renewable energy. By staying informed and adaptable, individuals and businesses can position themselves at the forefront of the next wave of economic expansion. As Albert Einstein once said, "In the midst of every crisis, lies great opportunity." By investing in these cutting-edge industries, you not only enhance your financial strategy but also contribute to a sustainable future. Remember, the path to wealth accumulation is paved with knowledge and foresight—stay curious, stay informed, and watch your investments flourish.

Chapter 13: Investing in Disruptive Innovations

Introduction

In today's rapidly evolving economy, investing in disruptive innovations has become a game-changer for both individuals seeking to boost their finances and businesses striving for growth. Disruptive technologies, which redefine industries and consumer behaviours, offer unique opportunities for those willing to embrace change and anticipate market shifts. This chapter will guide you through the essential strategies for identifying these pioneering companies, enabling you to make informed investment decisions that align with emerging trends. By understanding the forces driving innovation and recognizing the potential of these transformative players, you can position yourself at the forefront of financial success in an increasingly competitive landscape.

Investing in Innovation: Your Path to Prosperity

In today's fast-paced economic landscape, mastering wealth accumulation is more vital than ever. This discussion focuses on effective strategies for individuals seeking to boost their finances and businesses aiming for growth. A key focus of our exploration is the concept of investing in disruptive innovations—companies that are reshaping industries and markets with their cutting-edge technologies.

This guide aims to present these strategies in a clear, structured manner, incorporating examples, benefits, and crucial findings to equip readers with the tools they need to thrive financially.

1. Understanding Disruptive Innovation

Definition: Disruptive innovation refers to technological advancements that significantly alter the way industries operate. These innovations often start small and eventually overtake established companies, changing market dynamics forever.

Key Points:

- Examples of Disruptive Innovations: Companies like Netflix disrupted the traditional television and film industry, while Uber transformed transportation.

- Significance: Understanding these innovations is crucial as they often represent untapped investment opportunities that can yield substantial returns.

Strategies:

- Research Emerging Trends: Follow tech news, industry reports, and consumer behaviour to identify rising trends.

- Engage with Industry Experts: Participate in webinars, conferences, and forums to gain insights from thought leaders.

Benefits:

- Early identification of disruptive technologies can lead to significant financial gains.

2. Identifying Potential Investment Opportunities

Strategies:

- Sector Analysis: Focus on industries known for innovation, such as technology, healthcare, and renewable energy.

- Company Evaluation: Look for companies with strong leadership, a clear vision, and a commitment to innovation.

Example:

- Tesla Inc.: Initially considered a risky investment, Tesla's innovative approach to electric vehicles and energy solutions has transformed it into a market leader, demonstrating the potential of investing in disruptive innovations.

Benefits:

- Investing in the right companies at the right time can maximize returns while minimizing risks associated with more traditional investments.

3. Diversification of Investments

Concept: Diversification involves spreading investments across various sectors and asset classes to reduce risk.

Strategies:

- Balanced Portfolio: Include a mix of stocks, bonds, and alternative investments.
- Invest in Funds: Consider mutual funds or ETFs that focus on disruptive technologies to gain broad exposure with less risk.

Example:

- ARK Innovation ETF (ARKK): This fund invests in companies involved in disruptive technologies like genomics, automation, and fintech, offering investors a diversified approach to capitalize on innovation.

Benefits:

- Reduces the impact of poor-performing investments, thereby safeguarding overall financial health.

4. Long-Term Mindset

Concept: Building wealth is often a long-term endeavour, especially when investing in disruptive innovations that may take time to mature.

Strategies:

- Hold Period: Adopt a buy-and-hold strategy for investments in disruptive companies.
- Regularly Review: Periodically assess your portfolio to ensure alignment with your long-term financial goals.

Example:

- Amazon: Early investors who adopted a long-term mindset benefited immensely as the company grew from an online book store to a global e-commerce giant.

Benefits:

- Allows you to ride out market volatility and benefit from the overall upward trend of innovative companies over time.

5. Risk Management

Concept: Understanding and managing risk is essential for any investor looking to grow their wealth.

Strategies:

- Set Clear Risk Tolerance: Determine how much risk you are willing to take based on your financial goals and time horizon.

- Use Stop-Loss Orders: Implementing stop-loss orders can help protect your investments from significant downturns.

Example:

- Startup Investments: Investing in early-stage companies can be risky, but employing proper due diligence and diversification can mitigate potential losses.

Benefits:

- Protects your investment capital while enabling you to pursue potentially high-reward opportunities.

6. Continuous Learning and Adaptation

Concept: The financial landscape is constantly evolving, making continuous learning crucial for long-term success.

Strategies:

- Stay Informed: Regularly read financial news, attend seminars, and participate in courses to stay updated on market trends.

- Network: Build relationships with other investors and financial professionals to share insights and strategies.

Example:

- Following Influencers: Many successful investors, like Warren Buffett, share valuable insights that can enhance your investment strategy.

Benefits:

- A well-informed investor can adapt to changes in the market, making timely adjustments to their portfolio for optimal performance.

Summary

Investing in disruptive innovations represents a powerful strategy for individuals and businesses seeking to enhance their financial standing. By understanding the nature of disruptive technologies, identifying promising companies, and employing effective investment strategies, readers can navigate the complexities of wealth accumulation with confidence.

This discussion has outlined essential strategies and insights to empower you on your financial journey. By embracing a proactive, informed, and diversified investment approach, you can unlock the potential of your financial future. Remember, the key to mastering the money game lies not just in making smart investments, but in cultivating a mindset geared towards growth, learning, and resilience in the face of challenges.

Key Takeaways

1. **Invest in Disruptive Technologies:** Focus on identifying companies that lead the way in disruptive innovations, as they have the potential to reshape entire industries and generate substantial returns.

2. **Stay Ahead of Market Trends:** Develop a keen understanding of emerging industry trends and shifts,

enabling you to make informed investment decisions that align with future market demands.

3. Diversify Your Portfolio: Mitigate risk by diversifying your investments across various sectors and asset classes, which helps protect against market volatility and enhances long-term financial stability.

4. Leverage Financial Education: Continuously educate yourself about financial principles and investment strategies, empowering you to navigate the complexities of wealth accumulation confidently.

5. Adopt a Growth Mindset: Embrace a mindset focused on innovation and growth, fostering a culture of adaptability within your business or personal finances to seize new opportunities as they arise.

Conclusion

In the dynamic landscape of finance, mastering wealth accumulation requires a keen eye for innovation and the courage to embrace disruption. As we navigate this journey, it's crucial to invest not just in companies, but in ideas that challenge the status quo. By focusing on disruptive technologies, such as artificial intelligence, renewable energy, and biotechnology, investors can position themselves at the forefront of the next wave of market evolution. Remember the words of Peter Drucker: "The best way to predict the future is to create it." As you explore these transformative opportunities, stay attuned to emerging trends and market shifts that signal the next big breakthrough. By doing so, you not only enhance your financial portfolio but also contribute to shaping a future filled with potential and prosperity.

Chapter 14: Building a Strong Professional Network

Introduction

In today's fast-paced business landscape, success often hinges on who you know as much as what you know. This chapter dives into the transformative power of networking, highlighting how forging meaningful connections can unlock new opportunities for growth and collaboration. We'll explore practical strategies for cultivating and maintaining professional relationships that not only enhance your visibility but also enrich your career or business. Whether you're an aspiring entrepreneur or a seasoned professional, mastering the art of networking will empower you to tap into a wealth of resources and insights that can propel you toward your financial goals.

Networking for Financial Growth

In the journey of financial growth, whether as an individual seeking to boost your finances or a business aiming for expansion, networking emerges as a crucial pillar. This discussion delves into the transformative power of building and maintaining professional relationships, offering actionable strategies, compelling examples, and valuable insights that can lead to new opportunities.

The Power of Networking

Networking is more than just exchanging business cards; it's about creating a web of relationships that can support your financial goals. When done effectively, networking can open doors to new clients, collaborations, and innovative ideas. The more connections you have, the more resources and insights you can tap into.

Benefits of a Strong Network

1. Access to Opportunities: A robust network can lead to job offers, partnerships, or investment opportunities. Many positions are filled through referrals rather than traditional job postings.

Example: A marketing consultant who regularly attends industry events may meet a startup founder looking for marketing help, leading to a lucrative contract.

2. Knowledge Sharing: Networking allows you to gain insights from others' experiences. Learning from peers can help you avoid pitfalls and adopt best practices.

Example: A small business owner might connect with a mentor who shares strategies on managing cash flow effectively.

3. Increased Visibility: Being active in your network increases your visibility in your industry. The more people know you and your work, the more likely they are to think of you when opportunities arise.

Example: A freelancer who consistently shares their work on social media and engages with their network is more likely to be recommended for projects.

Effective Networking Strategies

To harness the full potential of networking, consider implementing the following strategies:

1. Attend Industry Events

Participate in conferences, seminars, and workshops relevant to your field. These gatherings are ripe for making connections.

- Tip: Prepare an elevator pitch to succinctly describe who you are and what you do. Make it engaging to leave a lasting impression.

2. Utilize Social Media

Platforms like LinkedIn, Twitter, and industry-specific forums are valuable tools for networking. Share content, engage in discussions, and connect with peers.

- Tip: Post valuable insights or articles related to your industry to position yourself as a thought leader.

3. Follow Up

After meeting someone, send a follow-up message to express your appreciation for the conversation. This helps solidify the connection and opens the door for future interactions.

- Example: If you meet someone at a conference, send a LinkedIn request with a personalized note referencing your discussion.

4. Join Professional Associations

Being part of industry-specific organizations can provide exclusive networking opportunities and resources.

- Benefit: Membership often grants access to events, webinars, and directories of other professionals in your field.

5. Leverage Existing Connections

Don't overlook your current network. Reach out to friends, family, or colleagues who might introduce you to others in your desired field.

- Observation: Personal connections often yield the most trustworthy referrals, as they come with built-in credibility.

Maintaining Your Network

Building a network is just the beginning; maintaining relationships is equally important. Here are key practices:

1. Regular Communication

Keep in touch with your contacts through occasional emails or social media interactions. Share updates about your progress and ask about theirs.

- Tip: Schedule reminders to check in with key connections periodically.

2. Offer Value

Networking should be a two-way street. Look for ways to help others in your network, whether through sharing resources, providing introductions, or offering expertise.

- Example: If you learn about a job opening that could suit a contact, share it with them. They'll remember your support when opportunities arise for you.

3. Be Genuine

Authenticity builds trust. Approach networking with a genuine desire to connect rather than just seeking personal gain.

- Observation: People are more likely to engage with you if they feel you are sincerely interested in building a relationship.

Summary

Building a strong professional network is an invaluable strategy for financial growth, whether as an individual or a business. By actively engaging with others, maintaining relationships, and offering value, you can create a thriving network that opens doors to new opportunities. Remember, in the world of networking, it's not just about who you know, but how well you cultivate those connections that truly matters. Embrace the journey, and watch as your network becomes a powerful asset in your financial success.

Key Takeaways

1. **Cultivate Genuine Relationships:** Focus on building authentic connections with others by showing genuine interest in their work and offering support where you can.

2. **Leverage Social Media:** Use platforms like LinkedIn to expand your reach, share valuable content, and engage with industry professionals to enhance your visibility.

3. **Attend Networking Events:** Actively participate in workshops, conferences, and local meetups to meet new people and establish face-to-face connections that can lead to collaboration.

4. **Follow Up and Stay Engaged:** Regularly check in with your contacts through messages or updates to maintain the relationship and remind them of your shared interests.

5. **Offer Value First:** Approach networking with a mindset of giving; share your knowledge, resources, or connections to foster goodwill and encourage reciprocation.

Conclusion

Building a strong professional network is essential for anyone looking to boost their finances or grow their business, as connections often open doors to new opportunities. Think of networking as planting seeds in a garden—nurturing relationships today can yield fruitful collaborations tomorrow. Start by attending industry events, engaging on social media, and reaching out to mentors; remember, it's not just about the number of contacts, but the quality of those relationships. As the saying goes, "Your network is your net worth." By investing time and effort into cultivating meaningful connections, you create a supportive ecosystem that fosters growth and innovation, ultimately leading to greater financial success and a thriving business landscape.

Chapter 15: Developing Effective Communication and Negotiation Skills

Introduction

In today's fast-paced business landscape, the ability to communicate effectively and negotiate with confidence can set you apart from the competition and propel your financial success. This chapter delves into the essential role of strong communication and negotiation skills, illustrating how they are not just tools but powerful assets in your journey toward wealth accumulation. By mastering these skills, you can foster meaningful relationships, navigate challenging conversations, and secure favourable outcomes that drive growth for both individuals and businesses alike. We'll explore practical strategies to refine your approach, ensuring that each interaction contributes to your overall success in a competitive market.

Mastering Communication and Negotiation for Financial Growth

In today's fast-paced business environment, strong communication and negotiation skills are vital for achieving success. They enable individuals and organizations to build relationships, foster collaboration, and navigate complex situations effectively. This discussion delves into the importance of these skills and offers practical strategies to refine them, ensuring you stand out in a competitive market.

The Importance of Communication Skills

1. Building Trust and Credibility

- Clear and honest communication fosters trust among colleagues, clients, and stakeholders.

- Example: Regularly updating your team on project developments shows transparency and builds confidence.
- Benefit: Trust enhances collaboration, leading to improved teamwork and productivity.

2. Enhancing Clarity and Understanding

- Effective Strategy: Use Simple Language
- Avoid jargon unless necessary; prioritize clarity to ensure your message is understood.
- Example: When presenting complex data, use visuals like charts to convey information effectively.
- Benefit: Clear communication reduces misunderstandings and minimizes errors.

3. Encouraging Open Dialogue

- Effective Strategy: Create a Safe Space for Feedback
- Encourage team members to share ideas and concerns without fear of repercussions.
- Example: Conduct regular brainstorming sessions where all opinions are valued.
- Benefit: Open dialogue leads to innovative solutions and a more engaged workforce.

The Power of Negotiation Skills

1. Achieving Win-Win Outcomes

- Effective negotiation is about finding solutions that benefit all parties involved.

- Effective Strategy: Focus on Interests, Not Positions
- Understand the underlying needs of all parties to create mutually beneficial agreements.
- Example: If negotiating salary, consider other benefits like flexible hours or professional development opportunities.
- Benefit: Win-win outcomes build stronger relationships and enhance long-term cooperation.

2. Mastering the Art of Persuasion

- Effective Strategy: Use the Principle of Reciprocity
- Offering value first can encourage others to reciprocate in negotiations.
- Example: Share useful resources or insights with clients, fostering goodwill and opening doors for future discussions.
- Benefit: Establishing goodwill can lead to more favourable negotiations down the line.

3. Developing Emotional Intelligence

- Understanding your emotions and those of others is crucial in negotiations.
- Effective Strategy: Practice Empathy
- Put yourself in the other party's shoes to understand their perspective better.
- Example: During negotiations, acknowledge the other party's concerns and validate their feelings.

- Benefit: Empathy can diffuse tension and foster collaboration, leading to more successful outcomes.

Strategies for Refining Communication Skills

1. Active Listening Techniques

    - Effective Strategy: Use Reflective Listening
    - Paraphrase what the other person has said to confirm understanding.
    - Example: "So what you're saying is that you're concerned about the project timeline, correct?"
    - Benefit: Active listening builds rapport and shows that you value the other person's input.

2. Non-verbal Communication Awareness

    - Effective Strategy: Monitor Body Language
    - Be aware of your own non-verbal cues and those of others.
    - Example: Maintain eye contact and open body posture to convey confidence and openness.
    - Benefit: Positive body language reinforces your message and fosters trust.

3. Tailoring Communication Style

    - Effective Strategy: Adapt to Your Audience
    - Assess the preferences of your audience and adjust your communication accordingly.
    - Example: Use technical language with experts but simplify terms for non-specialists.

- Benefit: Tailoring your approach enhances engagement and ensures your message resonates.

Enhancing Negotiation Skills

1. Preparation is Key

   - Effective Strategy: Research Thoroughly Before Negotiating
   - Understand market conditions, the other party's needs, and your own objectives.
   - Example: Gather data on industry standards to support your position in salary negotiations.
   - Benefit: Thorough preparation boosts your confidence and positions you for success.

2. Practicing Negotiation Scenarios

   - Effective Strategy: Role-Playing Exercises
   - Engage in mock negotiations to practice and refine your skills.
   - Example: Simulate a negotiation with a colleague, switching roles to gain different perspectives.
   - Benefit: Role-playing enhances your adaptability and prepares you for real-world situations.

3. Learning from Experience

   - Effective Strategy: Reflect on Past Negotiations
   - Analyze what worked and what didn't after each negotiation.

- Example: Keep a negotiation journal to track strategies and outcomes.
- Benefit: Continuous reflection helps you learn and improve over time.

Summary

Effective communication and negotiation skills are indispensable tools for achieving business success. By focusing on building trust, enhancing clarity, and fostering open dialogue, you can create stronger relationships. Simultaneously, mastering negotiation techniques, practicing empathy, and preparing thoroughly will empower you to secure favourable outcomes. Embrace these strategies, and watch as your interactions become more impactful and your business flourishes in a competitive landscape.

Key Takeaways

1. Master the Art of Listening: Successful communication starts with active listening, allowing you to understand needs and build stronger relationships with clients and partners.

2. Negotiate Win-Win Solutions: Strive for outcomes that benefit all parties, fostering trust and long-term collaborations that can lead to sustained financial growth.

3. Craft Clear Messages: Simplify complex ideas into clear, concise messages to ensure your value proposition resonates with your audience and drives engagement.

4. Build Confidence Through Preparation: Equip yourself with knowledge and practice to enhance your negotiation

skills, which empowers you to approach discussions with assurance and authority.

5. **Adapt Your Style to Your Audience:** Tailor your communication approach to suit different stakeholders, enhancing rapport and effectiveness in negotiations across various contexts.

Conclusion

In the journey to financial success, whether as an individual or a business, mastering the art of communication and negotiation is essential; as the saying goes, "It's not just what you say, but how you say it." By honing these skills, you not only build strong relationships but also open doors to opportunities that can significantly boost your financial growth. Implementing clear, empathetic communication and strategic negotiation techniques will empower you to navigate the competitive landscape effectively, leading to better deals, collaborations, and ultimately, wealth accumulation. Embrace these strategies, and watch as your financial landscape transforms, proving that the ability to connect and negotiate is just as crucial as the numbers on your balance sheet.

Chapter 16: Evaluating Investment Risks

Introduction

In the world of investing and business growth, understanding risk is essential for success. This chapter, "Evaluating Investment Risks," takes you on a journey through the different types of risks that can impact your financial decisions, whether you're an individual looking to boost your savings or a business striving for expansion. We'll explore practical techniques for assessing these risks, helping you to identify your own risk tolerance and make informed choices that align with your financial goals. By the end, you'll be equipped with the knowledge to navigate the uncertainties of investment, turning potential challenges into opportunities for growth.

Risk and Reward: Navigating Investment for Wealth Building

Investing can be a powerful way to build wealth, but it comes with its share of risks. Understanding these risks is crucial for both individuals looking to boost their finances and businesses aiming for growth. This discussion delves into the various risks associated with investments and business ventures, offering effective strategies, examples, and observations to help you navigate this complex landscape.

Understanding Investment Risks

1. Types of Risks

a. Market Risk

Market risk, or systemic risk, refers to the potential losses due to fluctuations in the overall market. Economic downturns, political instability, and global events can cause significant shifts.

Example: During the 2008 financial crisis, many investors faced steep losses as stock prices plummeted across the board.

b. Credit Risk

This risk arises from the possibility that a borrower may default on their obligations. For individuals, this could be a credit card company or a personal loan; for businesses, it can involve clients failing to pay their invoices.

Example: If a company extends credit to a customer who subsequently files for bankruptcy, it risks losing the revenue owed.

c. Liquidity Risk

Liquidity risk is the danger that an asset cannot be quickly converted into cash without a significant loss in value. This is particularly relevant in real estate or niche markets.

Example: Selling a property may take time, and if you need cash urgently, you might have to accept a lower price.

d. Operational Risk

This risk stems from internal processes, systems, or human errors. It can affect any organization, from small startups to large corporations.

Example: A software bug in an online trading platform could lead to significant financial losses for investors relying on that system.

Risk Assessment Techniques

1. Risk Tolerance

Understanding your risk tolerance is vital. It helps you decide how much risk you are comfortable taking on. This can vary greatly between individuals and businesses, influenced by factors such as age, financial goals, and current financial situation.

Assessment Strategy:

- Questionnaires: Utilize risk assessment questionnaires that gauge your comfort level with various investment scenarios.
- Historical Analysis: Look at how you reacted to past market downturns to better understand your emotional and financial resilience.

2. Diversification

Diversification is a powerful strategy to mitigate risks. By spreading your investments across various asset classes (stocks, bonds, real estate), you reduce the impact of a poor-performing investment on your overall portfolio.

Example: Instead of investing all your money in tech stocks, consider adding some bonds or international stocks to your portfolio.

3. Regular Review and Rebalancing

Regularly reviewing your investment portfolio is essential for managing risk. Market conditions change, and your asset allocation may need adjustments.

Strategy:

- Annual Reviews: Set aside time each year to assess your portfolio's performance and make necessary adjustments.

- Rebalancing: If stocks outperform bonds, your portfolio may become too heavily weighted in stocks. Rebalancing helps maintain your desired risk profile.

Benefits of Effective Risk Management

1. Enhanced Decision-Making

Understanding risks equips you with the knowledge to make informed investment decisions. You can weigh potential rewards against the risks more effectively.

2. Increased Confidence

When you comprehend the risks associated with your investments, you are less likely to panic during market fluctuations. This confidence can lead to better long-term results.

3. Financial Stability

Effective risk management can protect your wealth during downturns, ensuring that your financial foundation remains strong. This stability is especially crucial for businesses, as it can impact long-term growth and sustainability.

Crucial Findings and Observations

1. The Importance of Education

One of the key takeaways is that knowledge is power. The more you understand about investment risks, the better equipped you will be to handle them. Continuous education whether through books, courses, or professional advice can significantly enhance your investment strategies.

2. The Role of Professional Advice

For many individuals and businesses, seeking advice from financial advisors can provide valuable insights into risk management. Advisors can help tailor strategies that align with your risk tolerance and financial goals.

3. Psychological Factors

Behavioural finance plays a significant role in investment decisions. Recognizing psychological biases, such as overconfidence or loss aversion, can help you make more rational investment choices.

Summary

Evaluating investment risks is an essential component of any successful financial strategy. By understanding the various types of risks, employing effective assessment techniques, and maintaining a diversified portfolio, you can enhance your financial resilience. Whether you are an individual looking to boost your finances or a business aiming for growth, mastering risk management will set you on a path toward sustainable wealth accumulation.

Key Takeaways

1. **Understand Your Risk Tolerance**: Recognize your personal comfort level with risk, as it guides your investment choices and helps you make informed decisions.

2. **Diversify Your Portfolio**: Spread your investments across different asset classes to minimize risk and reduce the impact of any single loss on your overall financial health.

3. **Conduct Thorough Research**: Evaluate potential investments by analyzing market trends, financial

statements, and economic indicators to make well-informed decisions.

4. Utilize Risk Assessment Techniques: Employ tools such as scenario analysis and sensitivity analysis to forecast potential outcomes and better understand the risks involved.

5. Stay Informed and Adaptable: Continuously monitor your investments and the market landscape, adjusting your strategies as needed to mitigate risks and seize new opportunities.

Conclusion

In navigating the intricate world of investments, recognizing and managing risk is paramount for anyone looking to enhance their financial future or drive business growth. By employing effective risk assessment techniques—such as diversification, scenario analysis, and regular portfolio reviews—you can tailor your investment strategy to align with your personal risk tolerance. Remember, as Warren Buffett wisely said, "Risk comes from not knowing what you're doing." Equip yourself with knowledge and understanding, and you'll be well on your way to mastering the money game. Embrace the journey of financial empowerment, knowing that every informed decision brings you closer to your goals.

Chapter 17: Implementing Risk Mitigation Strategies

Introduction

In the ever-evolving landscape of finance, understanding how to safeguard your wealth is just as crucial as growing it. This chapter, "Implementing Risk Mitigation Strategies," delves into practical approaches that empower individuals and businesses alike to minimize financial and operational risks. By exploring essential tools like insurance, the benefits of diversification, and the importance of contingency planning, you'll gain insights that not only protect your assets but also enhance your overall financial resilience. Whether you're a savvy investor or a budding entrepreneur, these strategies will equip you with the knowledge to navigate uncertainties and build a more secure future.

Strategies for Wealth Accumulation and Risk Control

In the quest for financial success, whether as an individual or a business, understanding and implementing effective wealth accumulation strategies is crucial. This guide explores key strategies, focusing on risk mitigation, to help you navigate the complex world of finance. With clear explanations and actionable insights, we'll empower you to make informed decisions that lead to sustainable growth.

1. Understanding Risk Mitigation

A) What is Risk Mitigation?

Risk mitigation involves strategies and practices aimed at reducing financial and operational risks. For individuals, this means safeguarding personal finances, while for businesses, it refers to protecting assets and ensuring long-term viability.

B) Why is it Important?

Risk mitigation is vital because it helps prevent significant financial losses that could derail your wealth accumulation journey. By identifying potential risks early and implementing strategies to address them, you can create a stable foundation for growth.

2. Key Strategies for Risk Mitigation

A. Insurance: Protecting What Matters

i) Overview

Insurance acts as a safety net, providing financial protection against unforeseen events.

ii) Types of Insurance

- Health Insurance: Covers medical expenses and protects against high healthcare costs.
- Life Insurance: Ensures financial support for your loved ones in case of untimely death.
- Property Insurance: Protects physical assets, such as homes and businesses, from damage or loss.
- Liability Insurance: Shields against legal claims resulting from accidents or negligence.

iii) Benefits

- Financial Security: Reduces the burden of unexpected expenses.
- Peace of Mind: Knowing you're covered allows for better focus on wealth-building activities.

iv) Example

Consider a small business owner who invests in liability insurance. If a customer gets injured on the premises, this insurance can cover legal fees and medical costs, preventing potential financial ruin.

B. Diversification: Spreading the Risk

i) Overview

Diversification involves spreading investments across various asset classes to reduce risk.

ii) How to Diversify

- Investment Portfolio: Mix stocks, bonds, real estate, and commodities.

- Business Ventures: Consider multiple income streams, such as side businesses or passive income sources.

iii) Benefits

- Reduced Volatility: A downturn in one area may be offset by gains in another.

- Increased Opportunities: Exposure to different sectors can lead to better overall returns.

iv) Example

An individual with a diverse portfolio might invest in technology stocks, real estate, and government bonds. If tech stocks underperform, gains from real estate can balance the losses.

C. Contingency Planning: Preparing for the Unexpected

i) Overview

Contingency planning is about having a proactive approach to potential challenges.

ii) Steps to Create a Contingency Plan

1. Identify Potential Risks: Analyze what could go wrong in your financial or operational strategies.

2. Develop Response Strategies: Outline actions to take if risks materialize, such as cash reserves or alternative suppliers.

3. Regularly Review and Update: As circumstances change, so should your plans.

iii) Benefits

- Quick Response: Being prepared allows for swift action, minimizing disruptions.

- Confidence: Knowing you have a plan in place reduces anxiety about potential setbacks.

iv) Example

A small business may face a sudden supply chain disruption. Having a contingency plan in place means the owner can quickly source alternative suppliers, ensuring continued operation.

3. Crucial Findings and Observations

A. The Interconnectedness of Strategies

Risk mitigation strategies are not standalone; they work best when combined. For instance, insurance can complement a diversification strategy by providing additional security for your assets.

B. The Importance of Education

Understanding financial products and strategies is essential. Individuals and businesses alike should invest time in learning about financial literacy to make informed choices.

C. Continuous Monitoring

The financial landscape is ever-changing. Regularly reviewing your risk mitigation strategies ensures they remain effective and relevant to your current situation.

Summary

Implementing risk mitigation strategies is essential for both individuals and businesses looking to boost their finances or drive growth. By leveraging insurance, diversification, and contingency planning, you can create a robust framework that protects against uncertainties and enhances your wealth accumulation journey. As you navigate this path, remember that knowledge, preparation, and adaptability are your greatest allies.

Key Takeaways

1. Understand Your Financial Landscape: Assess your current financial situation thoroughly to identify strengths, weaknesses, and areas for improvement that can guide your wealth-building strategies.

2. Diversify Your Investments: Spread your investments across various assets and sectors to reduce risk and enhance potential returns, ensuring that you're not overly reliant on a single source of income.

3. Utilize Insurance Wisely: Protect your assets and income by investing in appropriate insurance policies that can

shield you from unexpected financial setbacks, providing peace of mind as you grow your wealth.

4. Develop a Contingency Plan: Prepare for uncertainties by creating a detailed plan that outlines steps to take in case of financial emergencies, ensuring you can maintain stability and continue on your path to wealth accumulation.

5. Regularly Review and Adjust Your Strategy: Periodically reassess your financial goals and strategies to adapt to changing circumstances and optimize your approach for sustained growth and risk management.

Conclusion

In the journey of wealth accumulation, implementing robust risk mitigation strategies is essential for both individuals and businesses striving for growth. By embracing tools like insurance to shield against unforeseen setbacks, diversifying investments to spread risk, and crafting contingency plans to navigate uncertainties, you create a safety net that allows for bolder financial decisions. As the saying goes, "Fortune favours the prepared mind." By proactively managing risks, you not only safeguard your current assets but also pave the way for sustainable success and resilience in a dynamic market. Remember, in mastering the money game, it's not just about chasing wealth; it's about building a secure foundation that empowers you to thrive, no matter the challenges ahead.

Chapter 18: Preparing for Economic Downturns

Introduction

In today's unpredictable economic landscape, being prepared for downturns is not just a luxury—it's a necessity for individuals and businesses alike. This chapter delves into the crucial role of contingency planning and financial preparedness, offering clear, actionable strategies to safeguard your assets and maintain stability when times get tough. By embracing a proactive mindset and implementing smart financial practices, you can build resilience that not only helps you weather storms but also positions you for growth when the economy rebounds. Let's explore how you can create a robust safety net that empowers you to thrive, no matter what challenges come your way.

Preparing for Economic Uncertainty

Economic downturns are inevitable, but how you prepare for them can make all the difference between thriving and merely surviving. This chapter delves into the vital strategies for maintaining financial stability and resilience, whether you're an individual looking to boost your finances or a business aiming for growth. Here's a comprehensive guide to effective contingency planning and financial preparedness.

Understanding Economic Downturns

Economic downturns are periods of reduced economic activity, often characterized by rising unemployment, declining consumer spending, and decreasing business investment. These can be triggered by various factors, including financial crises, global events, or even shifts in consumer behaviour. Recognizing the signs of an impending downturn can give you a head start in preparing.

Key Indicators of a Downturn

1. Rising Unemployment Rates: A spike in job losses can signal economic trouble.

2. Decreased Consumer Spending: When people cut back on purchases, businesses often follow suit.

3. Falling Stock Markets: A downturn in stock performance can indicate broader economic issues.

Strategies for Individuals

1. Build an Emergency Fund

a) What It Is: An emergency fund is savings set aside for unexpected expenses or loss of income.

b) How to Build It: Aim for three to six months' worth of living expenses. Start small by saving a percentage of each pay check until you reach your goal.

c) Benefits: This fund acts as a financial cushion, allowing you to navigate tough times without falling into debt.

2. Diversify Income Streams

a) What It Is: Generating income from multiple sources reduces reliance on a single pay check.

b) How to Implement: Consider side gigs, freelance work, or investments in rental properties or stocks.

c) Benefits: Diversification helps maintain financial stability even if one income source falters.

3. Cut Unnecessary Expenses

a) What It Is: Review your monthly expenses and identify non-essential items.

b) How to Do It: Create a budget and categorize your spending. Look for subscriptions, dining out, or luxury items that can be reduced or eliminated.

c) Benefits: Cutting costs frees up cash for savings and emergency funds, enhancing your financial resilience.

Strategies for Businesses

1. Conduct a Financial Audit

a) What It Is: Analyzing your current financial position helps identify strengths and weaknesses.

b) How to Conduct It: Review cash flow statements, profit margins, and expenditure reports. Look for areas of overspending or underperforming products.

c) Benefits: This audit provides clarity on where to cut costs and where to invest for future growth.

2. Strengthen Your Cash Flow Management

a) What It Is: Effective cash flow management ensures that you have enough liquidity to cover obligations.

b) How to Enhance It: Implement strategies like faster invoicing, stricter credit policies, and negotiating better payment terms with suppliers.

c) Benefits: Improved cash flow means your business can survive periods of reduced sales and maintain operations.

3. Build Strong Relationships with Customers

a) What It Is: A loyal customer base can be a business's most valuable asset.

b) How to Foster Loyalty: Engage with customers through personalized communication, loyalty programs, and excellent customer service.

c) Benefits: Loyal customers are more likely to continue purchasing during downturns, providing a steadier revenue stream.

Contingency Planning

1. Create a Contingency Plan

a) What It Is: A detailed plan that outlines steps to take in response to specific downturn scenarios.

b) How to Develop It: Identify potential risks (e.g., economic downturns, supply chain disruptions) and create action plans for each. Include communication strategies, financial measures, and operational adjustments.

c) Benefits: A solid contingency plan equips you to respond swiftly and effectively when challenges arise, minimizing disruption.

2. Regularly Review and Update Plans

a) What It Is: Ensuring your contingency plan stays relevant in a changing environment.

b) How to Execute: Schedule quarterly reviews to assess and update your plans based on current economic conditions and business performance.

c) Benefits: Keeping your plan current ensures you are always prepared, reducing stress during actual downturns.

Summary

Preparation is key to thriving in the face of economic downturns. By building a robust financial foundation, diversifying income streams, and developing comprehensive contingency plans, both individuals and businesses can enhance their resilience. Remember, the goal isn't just to survive; it's to emerge stronger, ready to capitalize on opportunities when the economy rebounds. With thoughtful strategies and proactive measures, you can navigate challenges with confidence and poise, ensuring financial stability and growth in the long run.

Key Takeaways

1. Establish an Emergency Fund: Save at least three to six months' worth of expenses to create a financial cushion that can sustain you during tough times.

2. Diversify Income Streams: Explore multiple sources of income, such as side hustles or investments, to reduce reliance on a single revenue stream.

3. Cut Unnecessary Expenses: Review your budget regularly and eliminate non-essential spending to improve cash flow and enhance financial flexibility.

4. Invest in Skills and Knowledge: Continuously upgrade your skills and education to increase your marketability and adaptability in changing economic conditions.

5. Create a Contingency Plan: Develop a detailed plan outlining steps to take during an economic downturn,

ensuring you are prepared to pivot and protect your finances.

Conclusion

In today's unpredictable economic landscape, preparing for downturns isn't just smart—it's essential. Contingency planning is your financial safety net, allowing both individuals and businesses to weather the storm when challenges arise. By building a robust emergency fund, diversifying income streams, and adopting a proactive mindset, you can transform potential setbacks into opportunities for growth. Remember, as Winston Churchill said, "Success is not final, failure is not fatal: It is the courage to continue that counts." Embrace resilience as your guiding principle, and you'll not only survive tough times but emerge stronger and more financially savvy.

Chapter 19: Exploring International Markets

Introduction

In today's interconnected world, the prospect of investing in international markets offers an exciting pathway to financial growth, yet it comes with its own set of challenges. This chapter will delve into the myriad benefits of diversifying your investment portfolio beyond borders, including access to emerging economies and the potential for higher returns. However, navigating the complexities of different economic environments requires a keen understanding of global market dynamics, cultural nuances, and geopolitical factors. By equipping yourself with strategic insights and practical tips, you'll be better prepared to seize opportunities while managing risks, setting the stage for sustainable wealth accumulation in a truly global landscape.

Unlocking Global Opportunities

Investing in international markets can be a game changer for individuals seeking to boost their finances and for businesses aiming for growth. This discussion delves into the benefits and challenges of global investments, offering insights and strategies to navigate diverse economic landscapes effectively.

The Benefits of Investing in International Markets

1. Diversification

    - Strategy: Diversifying your investment portfolio by including international assets.
    - Example: An investor holds stocks from both domestic and international companies, reducing the risk tied to local economic downturns.

- Benefits: Diversification helps to mitigate risk. If one market suffers, others may thrive, leading to more stable overall returns.

2. Access to Emerging Markets

    - Strategy: Targeting high-growth economies, such as India or Brazil.
    - Example: A business invests in a tech startup in Southeast Asia, tapping into rapid digital adoption.
    - Benefits: Emerging markets often provide greater growth potential compared to mature markets, leading to higher returns.

3. Hedging Against Inflation

    - Strategy: Investing in foreign assets that may appreciate during inflationary periods.
    - Example: Buying commodities or real estate in countries with stable economies.
    - Benefits: This strategy can protect the purchasing power of your investments, as different economies experience inflation differently.

4. Broader Economic Insights

    - Strategy: Studying global trends and economic indicators.
    - Example: A business observes shifts in consumer behaviour across markets to adjust its marketing strategy.
    - Benefits: Gaining insights from multiple economies can enhance decision-making and strategic planning.

The Challenges of International Investing

1. Currency Risk

    - Challenge: Fluctuations in exchange rates can affect returns.
    - Mitigation: Using currency hedging strategies.
    - Observation: A U.S. investor may lose money if the dollar strengthens against a foreign currency, even if the foreign investment performs well.

2. Political and Economic Instability

    - Challenge: Investments in politically unstable regions can lead to significant losses.
      Mitigation: Conduct thorough country risk assessments.
    - Observation: A business must evaluate the political climate before entering a new market to avoid potential upheavals.

3. Regulatory Differences

    - Challenge: Navigating different legal and regulatory environments.
    - Mitigation: Seeking local legal counsel and compliance expertise.
    - Observation: Understanding local laws can prevent costly missteps and fines.

4. Cultural Barriers

    - Challenge: Misunderstanding local customs and consumer behaviour.

- Mitigation: Investing in market research and local partnerships.
- Observation: A company may fail if it overlooks cultural nuances, leading to poor product acceptance.

Effective Global Investment Strategies

1. Invest in International ETFs

   - Description: Exchange-Traded Funds (ETFs) allow investors to buy a basket of international stocks.
   - Benefits: Lower costs and easier access to global markets compared to buying individual stocks.

2. Utilize Professional Investment Managers

   - Description: Hiring investment managers who specialize in global markets.
   - Benefits: Their expertise can enhance investment decisions and risk management.

3. Adopt a Long-term Perspective

   - Description: Focusing on long-term growth rather than short-term gains.
   - Benefits: This strategy allows for the natural growth of investments in response to global economic trends.

4. Monitor Global Trends

   - Description: Keeping an eye on international news, economic reports, and market analyses.

- Benefits: Being informed helps in making timely investment decisions.

Summary

Investing in international markets offers a wealth of opportunities for both individuals and businesses. By understanding the benefits and challenges, and implementing effective strategies, you can navigate the complexities of global investing. Embrace the potential of international markets to enhance your financial growth and secure a prosperous future. The journey may be challenging, but the rewards can be substantial for those who approach it with knowledge and diligence.

Key Takeaways

1. Diversification Benefits: Investing in international markets can diversify your portfolio, reducing risk and potentially increasing returns by tapping into different economic cycles.

2. Cultural Understanding: Successful global investments require a deep understanding of local cultures and business practices, which can help you make informed decisions and build strong relationships.

3. Economic Awareness: Awareness of varying economic environments is crucial; understanding factors like inflation rates and political stability can significantly impact your investment outcomes.

4. Currency Considerations: Fluctuations in currency exchange rates can affect your returns, so it's vital to consider hedging strategies to protect your investments from currency risks.

5. **Long-Term Perspective:** Approaching international investments with a long-term mindset can help you navigate short-term volatility and capitalize on the growth potential of emerging markets.

Conclusion

Investing in international markets opens doors to diverse opportunities and can significantly enhance your financial growth, but it's essential to navigate the complexities of different economic environments. As you explore these global landscapes, remember the wise words of Peter Drucker: "The best way to predict the future is to create it." By understanding varying market dynamics and cultural nuances, you can make informed decisions that bolster your portfolio. Embrace the potential of international investments while staying aware of the associated risks; this balanced approach will not only strengthen your financial strategy but also cultivate resilience against market fluctuations. In this interconnected world, your success lies in being both bold and informed—ready to seize opportunities wherever they arise.

Chapter 20: Adapting to Consumer Preferences and Market Dynamics

Introduction

In today's fast-paced world, the key to financial success—whether for individuals or businesses—lies in the ability to adapt swiftly to evolving consumer preferences and shifting market dynamics. This chapter explores the vital importance of agility, urging you to embrace flexibility and innovation as cornerstones of your strategy. By staying attuned to what your customers truly want and being ready to pivot when necessary, you can not only safeguard your financial future but also seize new opportunities for growth. Let's unlock the secrets to thriving in a landscape that's constantly changing, ensuring you remain competitive and prosperous in your financial journey.

Navigating Market Trends and Consumer Preferences

In today's fast-paced financial landscape, whether you're an individual looking to boost your finances or a business aiming for growth, mastering the principles of wealth accumulation is essential. This guide delves into the dynamic interplay of consumer preferences and market dynamics, providing effective strategies, examples, and crucial insights to help you navigate these changes successfully.

1. Understanding Consumer Preferences

Strategy: Continuous Market Research

a) Effective Approach: Regularly conduct surveys, focus groups, and analyze social media trends to gain insights into consumer behaviour.

b) Example: A clothing retailer could use social media analytics to track trending styles and adjust inventory accordingly.

c) Benefits: This strategy ensures that your offerings align with consumer desires, enhancing customer satisfaction and loyalty.

d) Key Insight: Staying attuned to consumer preferences is not a one-time effort. It's an ongoing commitment that requires businesses to adapt their offerings in real time.

2. Embracing Flexibility in Business Operations

Strategy: Agile Business Models

a) Effective Approach: Adopt an agile business model that allows for rapid adjustments to product lines or service offerings based on market feedback.

b) Example: A tech company that initially focused on hardware can pivot to software solutions if customer demand shifts.

c) Benefits: Flexibility in operations can lead to faster response times, reduced risks, and increased market share.

d) Key Insight: Agility not only helps in meeting current demands but also positions businesses to anticipate future trends, creating a proactive rather than reactive approach.

3. Innovating Product and Service Offerings

Strategy: Foster a Culture of Innovation

a) Effective Approach: Encourage employees at all levels to contribute ideas for new products or improvements.

b) Example: Google's "20% Time" allows employees to spend a portion of their work week on projects they're passionate about, leading to innovations like Gmail.

c) Benefits: A culture of innovation fosters creativity and can result in breakthrough products that resonate with consumers.

d) Key Insight: Innovation should not be limited to product development; it can also apply to customer service, marketing strategies, and operational efficiencies.

4. Leveraging Technology for Growth

Strategy: Invest in Digital Transformation

a) Effective Approach: Utilize technology to enhance customer experience, streamline operations, and gather data.

b) Example: E-commerce platforms can implement AI chatbots to provide 24/7 customer support, improving engagement and sales.

c) Benefits: Technology can significantly reduce costs, improve efficiency, and create a more personalized experience for consumers.

d) Key Insight: Investing in the right technology not only supports immediate business goals but also lays the groundwork for future scalability.

5. Building Strong Customer Relationships

Strategy: Personalized Marketing

a) Effective Approach: Use data analytics to tailor marketing messages to individual customer preferences.

b) Example: Netflix analyzes viewing habits to recommend shows, resulting in higher user engagement and satisfaction.

c) Benefits: Personalized experiences lead to stronger customer loyalty and can drive repeat purchases.

d) Key Insight: Customers are more likely to engage with brands that understand and cater to their unique needs and preferences.

6. Financial Literacy and Wealth Management

Strategy: Educate Yourself and Your Team

a) Effective Approach: Regularly invest in financial education to understand market dynamics and wealth accumulation strategies.

b) Example: Attend workshops, webinars, and read financial literature to stay informed about investment options and economic trends.

c) Benefits: Increased financial literacy empowers individuals and businesses to make informed decisions that enhance wealth.

d) Key Insight: Understanding financial concepts not only aids in personal wealth management but also equips business leaders to navigate economic fluctuations confidently.

Summary

Adapting to consumer preferences and market dynamics is crucial for both individuals and businesses seeking to thrive in today's environment. By embracing flexibility, fostering innovation, leveraging technology, and building strong customer relationships, you can position yourself for sustainable growth and wealth accumulation. The key is to remain agile and open to change, continually learning and evolving in response to the ever-shifting landscape. In mastering the money game, your ability to adapt and innovate will be your greatest asset.

Key Takeaways

1. Stay Agile: To thrive in a fast-changing market, businesses must quickly adapt their strategies based on shifting consumer preferences and emerging trends.

2. Embrace Innovation: Continuously seek creative solutions and new ideas that resonate with your audience, ensuring your offerings remain relevant and appealing.

3. Customer-Centric Approach: Prioritize understanding your customers' needs and feedback, as this insight is crucial for refining products and services to enhance satisfaction.

4. Flexible Planning: Develop adaptable business plans that allow for quick pivots when unexpected market changes occur, maintaining your competitive edge.

5. Data-Driven Decisions: Utilize analytics and market research to make informed choices, ensuring that your strategies align with consumer behaviours and preferences for optimal growth.

Conclusion

To thrive in today's fast-paced financial landscape, whether as an individual or a business, it's essential to stay agile and responsive to ever-evolving consumer preferences and market dynamics. Embracing flexibility not only fosters innovation but also positions you to capitalize on emerging opportunities. As the adage goes, "In the midst of chaos, there is also opportunity," and by adapting your strategies, you can turn challenges into stepping stones for growth. Ultimately, mastering the money game means staying attuned to your audience and being willing to pivot when necessary, ensuring your financial journey is both resilient and rewarding.